KARLA KLEAR SKY

A METH ADDICT'S MOTHER'S MEMOIR

KARLA V. GARRISON

Three Tears

Thanks to the following for permission to quote or reprint:
Leonard Pitts Jr., Pulitzer-Prize winning columnist for the Miami Herald.
Charisma, March 1988
McCall's, May 2000
All rights reserved.
Also, many thanks to Joshua Garrison for allowing his story to be told.

This book was written for parents of alcoholics/addicts.
It is meant to comfort and empower.
The story is true, but the message is entirely the opinion of the author's.
She is not a medical doctor or chemical dependency professional;
therefore, the suggestions are intended to be helpful and encouraging but
not advice.
The author and publisher disclaim any responsibility for any liability, loss
or risk, in any form, which happens as a result, directly or indirectly, of
any of the material contained in this book.

Author's note.
This memoir is a true and personal account of actual experiences. Some
paraphrasing and quotes are left uncited to protect the anonymity of the
men and women who shared their experience, strength and hope.

Library of Congress Cataloging-in-Publication data.

Karla Klear Sky: A Meth Addict's Mother's Memoir/ Karla V. Garrison
p.   cm.
ISBN 1440462011
1. Addiction—Family relationships
2. Addiction—Co-dependency
3. Co-dependency—Memoir
4. Co-dependency—Recovery I Title.

Cover design by Ken Campbell

www.karlaklearsky.com

This book is dedicated to our beloved son Joshua, anyone chemically dependent and written for all parents in pain.

ACKNOWLEDGEMENTS

Thanks to everyone who honored this work with their kind support. First to God, for sustaining us, to Bob, my amazing husband and publishing partner, for surviving not only our son's addiction but my obsession. To my mentor and friend, Willie Lippmann and marvelous writer and published author, for his encouragement, knowledge and insight. To my agent, Neil Salkind, for his enthusiasm and belief in the project, to Pat Sory for typing the original manuscript from over eight hundred hand written pages and to Leonard Pitts Jr., a generous celebrity and champion.

Also heartfelt thanks to: my beloved mother, Vivian, who taught me I could do anything, to my precious sons, Jason and Joshua, for their unconditional support and to my wonderful aunt, Billy Angstadt and dear and astute friends, Susie Schaeberle, for her tender care, deep understanding and extraordinary assistance and to Helen Boody for her careful and thorough critique and encouragement.

Many thanks too, for all the readers and friends who gave helpful feedback: The wonderful Olympia Writer's Round Table, Sandy Ckodre, Becky Durkin, Chris Clark, Carol Cooke, Loranne Schmidt, Flemming Behrend, Pat Temple, Nancy Stoops, Becky Wagner and others. The talented WWW's (Wild Women Writers) Katherine Alderete, Marcella Bateman, Darcy Cline, Joan Cronk, Kristina Sullivan, Barbara Swayze and especially the gifted and benevolent Laura Kepner for her abiding support.

Also grateful thanks to Al-Anon and to a host of others who intersected this project: My dear and wise friends, Marge Bethel and Des Thomson, dear friend,

Mary Ann Roberts, Kim Anderson of Safe Streets Tacoma, Michael Darcher of Pierce College, my funny and candid friend, Joannie Cole, talented musician and screen writer, Gary Davis and his wife Gayle, humorous writer, Edd Johnson and his wife Holly, Ralph and Colleen Thomson and Carrie Boulet for their sustained interest, Robyn West for special support and understanding and to Lizzy Shannon, Judith Capili, Ketra Emberton and "The Henchmen of Enumclaw" for cracking the whip and dearest and oldest friend, Phyllis Papagiannis. Thanks also to authors: Peggy Vincent, Victoria Strauss, Susan Shaughnessy, Judith Rich Harris, Chris Volkman and the witty iconoclast, Gerard Jones, for his expansive website where I found my literary agent.

What have I learned? There are more discouragers than encouragers, but when watered, seeds grow into strong stalks. Sincerest thanks for those who helped when I sunk into the darkest corner, you pulled me up to shake my fist at the beast and push on.

CONTENTS

PROLOGUE

Parents are in bed but cannot sleep. Their hollow eyes stare into addiction, a pandemic that nibbles from within and steams the curl from their souls.

I know because I am the good, but flawed, mother of a drug addict. For nine years I've clawed out of pain. This true story is about addiction, a monster that splays lives across generations and spears them into tainted and sullied futures.

If you are in pain, I understand what you're up against and how you are hurting and searching. I know your child is spiraling out of control and maybe you are, too. I know you ask yourself what went wrong. And I know the incandescent rage, but also the love and dull ache in your heart.

Parent pain is real and profound. Parents are held responsible for children's behaviors and are vilified or glorified accordingly. We can take some, but not all credit for good and bad outcomes. When children turn out well, parents feel everything from puffed pride to satisfaction or sheer relief. Successful offspring can tend to the old or at least stand on their own.

But when children are addicts, they drag you down and keep you down while staying down themselves. But this monster is a disease, not the result of poor parenting. You didn't cause it, although many will point a finger. You can't prevent, cure or control it but you can survive, even flourish in spite of it.

Are you a parent in pain? I offer you my experience and hope. This book is for you—not for your child or others unscathed by addiction. I don't have all the answers or even all of the questions, but I will share what helped me not only endure, but also prevail. But how do we bear the sorrow? The goal is to answer that question: to hold out one hand to lift you up and another to help you through. You are not alone. I share your fears and know how your heart is broken. Denial numbs and renders us ineffective. We resist knowing because someone explained, knowing is worse than suspicion, which leaves a gate open for escape.

Perhaps like me, you practiced parenting diligently for what you thought would be a joyous venture. And you too, were lulled into ignorance and bliss that evaporated when all hell broke loose.

The disease plays no favorites. It's an equal opportunist taking up residence in families from all backgrounds. No one's bigger or stronger than drugs. Addiction will take anyone down this yawning grave.

This confessional is my gift to you. Whatever help it can offer I give it with tears in my eyes for I know your story is much like mine. I know your pain. I feel it and also hope you feel my empathy reach out across these pages. Right where you are sitting or standing, right here, right now, many suffer the same battle. There are millions of addicts and millions of parents also doing hard time. You pass them on the street, see them in stores and work next to them for years with their heartache disguised. I invite you into my private world because I'm one of them and perhaps you are, too. This book offers a soft place to fall. Imagine fewer struggles. Imagine living every moment from a place of love instead of fear.

Come; let me take your hand. We will find our way out together. Let me wrap loving, nonjudgmental arms around you, validate your pain and coax you back to life.

Nine, pronounced "ku," in Japanese, is a homonym for pain and suffering.

ONE

Beast Unleashed

1993 – 1997

I stand in the kitchen next to the counter. My eyes are puffy from last night's sobs. I breathe through my mouth because my nose is still swollen and raw and grotesque like our lives all twisted and clogged. My hand trembles when it finds the knife. It shakes with happiness just thinking of it: popping the skin, under my gown, scraping a bone and jabbing the flesh.

I imagine the thirst as I bleed on the floor and the icy cold and lovely darkness. I float to the ceiling and look down where she lies with a smile on her face, all white and wet, with wonderful red spreading everywhere.

But we weren't always crazy.

Before the disease gutted us like fish we were normal. But home, once a tranquil refuge, became a nightmare. I sigh remembering when we were parents who were best friends and lovers who adored their two happy sons. It was a good life—ordinary, comfortable and sane.

Leaving the building where I work, I beat back fear with today's satisfaction. The Army Family Advocacy program at Fort Lewis, Washington, contracts with a local college where I teach. This afternoon's group of domestic violence perpetrators rewards my training as a mental health counselor. Breaking defenses and building rapport is my strong suit, and this morning's briefing for three hundred soldiers on spouse abuse awareness is a favorite opportunity to strut my stuff in a one-woman show. Pumped and proud, I neatly load belongings into the silver Volvo and start home. But before getting off Post the glow fades.

I drive east. Mount Rainier stands glorious in the welcome sun. Fresh snow anoints the slopes leaving her pristine and white disguising her flaws beneath the powder. The mountain seems close, but is miles away like the happier times of our lives. I flip on the radio to shake the worries and swallow hard. Today is the first day back to school after winter break and there will be hell to pay. Squinting, I ponder this morning's exchange with seventeen-year-old Joshua, "Come straight home after school and do your homework," I ask. "Get off my case!" he yells, slamming the door.

Maybe the hell will be quiet hell, where he only stares into space and wishes we both were dead. Not hell that smears rooms with screams in faces and words that slash like running chain saws.

I arrive home and find him asleep sprawled on the couch reeking of sweat and insolence. Waking the viper is dicey.

"Please get up Joshua, shower and start your homework." God forbid. Quick, handcuffs and a padded cell, and while you're at it a public flogging and a scarlet 'P' for Psycho. Not for him of course, but me—me the mother. Because after all if it weren't for omission or commission, how could a boy morph into a flicking serpent?

Have we tried talking to him in a gentle voice? The world's accusations echo in my head. *Family dinners, Sunday school, Scouts and sports? Have we given guidance, love and boundaries?* No, of course not. We tuned out and gave up. Not likely. How dare they point a finger? There's a prevailing notion rotten parents derail their little "darlins." Yet, there may be modicum of truth behind the theory and it's that ascription that crowds our heart and cries us to sleep.

But Bob and I are faithful stewards. We've taught our sons right from wrong and set good examples. Still in spite of

2

our best efforts, we have this child who smashes every value laid before him. Joshua was a star athlete and scholar, a kind and loving magnet who drew people to him with an electric smile as big as his warm heart...a sweet little boy who left love notes on my pillow and hugged me hard and long. But now he's a stranger.

You know something's wrong when you dread coming home. When you don't hit the door and kick off your shoes but run for the toilet and spray brown water into the pot. When you don't ask your kid about his day but want to grab his throat and slam him into the wall. When you want to slap his face and stomp and screech until your brains drip from the ceiling.

Joshua slipped away but we thought it was emancipation. Although he was mouthy, things were fine.

Then something changed.

Of course it was drug behavior but we didn't know it. It started from thirteen and ushered the darkness. He slid into experimentation with the usual suspects: beer, pot and shrooms picked from suburban lawns. But what began as thumbing his nose slowly escalated to thready turmoil and recreation moved to obsession. As he disappeared into addiction it took us with him.

Now four years later, Joshua is flunking history and barely passing English. We encourage education and yet we have an older son, although bright with Attention Deficit Disorder (ADD), and now Joshua also smart and promising, barely scraping by.

A change in personality and school performance is classic. But for green rookies, it's easy to confuse common problems with real danger signs. Even experienced parents deny the obvious and who can blame them? Who wouldn't delay a plunge into terror?

The most awful moments are pushed from clear consciousness. I can't recall every detail because to dig deep is to go there and some places should never be revisited. Wary, I draw closer compelled to investigate but hang back a little because to know will command me to act.

I hear Jason, our twenty- year- old son, upstairs on the phone. Something in his inflection warns me. I tiptoe to his room when it becomes clear this argument's different. The boys, like all brothers, have had their battles—some brutal, most ordinary—but through it all their love and devotion remained solid. But now Jason's voice races with desperation.

"No, Joshua! This shit will mess you up!" Jason yells into the receiver. "No, no, Joshua! Mom and dad *ARE* going to hear about this. Stop denying—stop trying to bullshit! Crank will fucking kill you!"

I open Jason's door. Relief flashes from his eyes. The burden shifts and although Joshua's enraged, it has to be confronted. Eventually you come face to face with addiction when life will never be the same.

Perhaps Joshua's falsely accused. We'll talk and deflect. Although stunned and shaken, we cling to elusive hope that somehow, someway, this isn't true. As long as we keep the secret and live in denial, we also keep the lie that hits us in the head while our throats are slit.

Their dad takes over when he hears the commotion and orders seventeen- year- old Joshua home. Fear pokes us in the chest and demands our silence. The monster's perched to swoop and descend as it drums its talons and clicks its teeth. The room is rank with evil and now a wicked shimmy. We retreat to corners. Closed in, the threat traps us in an airless box. We wait alone with our private torments as the apprehension grows. No one speaks. No one makes a sound. We sit very still and very straight. Like rabbits in a thicket, with a coven of circling hawks, I wonder who will be snatched first and torn apart. Collared with dry mouths, time crawls. Life stops. Then Joshua blasts through the front door.

4

"This is bullshit!" he announces.

"Sit down and let's discuss this," Bob says.

"You want me to tell some shit on you?" Joshua says, pointing at his brother.

My heart pounds and I pace with fingers clasped beneath my chin. One hand drops to a shoulder to scratch an itch until it bleeds. Guts churn and beg bowels to evacuate. Jason coughs. Bob sniffs and clears his throat. We plumb the depths but come up empty. Bare and defenseless, we stand exposed to the sinister force. Words fly like furniture lifted by poltergeist. Objects go in and out of focus as sounds muffle, then amplify, like the strain from a cracked car window. Light headed and woozy, I'm outside my body and can't comprehend. I look down, then up and then climb on the coffee table and scream into his face, "Joshua, if you're using crank I'll cut your heart out!"

Mad with hunger, the beast devours without conscience or regret. The fiend thunders past, smashing souls and blowing dreams to ashes. With one twitch, it turns solid ground to quicksand, unhinges its jaw and swallows you whole.

To be in the presence of meth madness is formidable. The face contorts, the voice transforms and the body both stiffens and shivers as the wave ripples across the soul and sucks the personage up and away. Transfixed and frozen, with eyes saying, *this can't be happening*, we could only stare in disbelief, for in that moment, we too we're transported along with the addict to the unbelievable.

"I'm not doing drugs! Joshua roars, his face burning with rage, spit flying with fury, as his hand clenches and slams full force into the family room floor. The bones crunch and crack as the sound ricochets across the room.

Quick, take cover, my inner voice warns. *Duck and brace*! It's now upon us; the demon's unleashed, a flash- over about to engulf us. *Run, run, faster, faster, hide, upstairs, yes upstairs. Hide, hide, under the pillow, muffle the growls, the screams, the breakage, the sounds!* It's shifting, moving outside —Bob, Jason, holding Joshua down—all screaming, cursing, crying— childlike, I huddle under blankets and whisper, "This is a madhouse—this is a madhouse."

We keep our first "secret" that night when the E.R. doctor asks how Joshua broke his hand. I think we all said rough housing with his brother. How could we say he was a meth addict who went into a maniacal rage? We couldn't talk about *that*, because that would make it real. Denial slid under the door and coiled on our chest while we slept.

Life goes into a skid when you least expect it. We're lucky it grabs us alone without an audience, without eyes bearing down with judgment. But soon after, the impersonal voice doesn't know or care we're mangled—just a phone call, another phone call…just doing their job.

The vice-principal speaks, "Are you aware Joshua has cut class for the third time and is facing a two-week out-of-school suspension?" I ask if she can call back an hour and a half later when Bob comes home. She snickers and catches herself saying she doubts she'll be around then. I quickly counter with a request for the next evening. Click. End of phone call. These rigid moments dip us into scalding water. The school calls more and more often to report Joshua is flunking, cutting, tardy or messing up somehow, some way. I'm terrified of the phone. Forget the royal stamp of approval, if a Polly or Peter perfect decrees success, a screw-up proves we're failures.

Now on speed dial with the school, Joshua's looking at another suspension, or we have wiggle room if he agrees to a drug/alcohol assessment. The mere mention leaves me shaken. Why not throw me into a wood chipper? But I skip over the fear with denial. Joshua yields with pressure and we sweat out the day. He scores "at risk" and needs eighteen hours of substance education awareness. No problem, but when we're about to leave the office, the counselor says there will be three mandatory urine analysis (U.A.) tests. Now Joshua freaks out. Jumping to his feet, he exclaims, "All deals are off!" and bolts from the building as we sit there stunned. Looking up, the wooden counselor says dully, "He's probably using more seriously than we assessed." Fear runs its blade down our backs.

Over and over and over again Joshua denies he's using. It's all a mistake of amazing proportions. Swallowed by despair, we want to believe him because we *need* to believe him. He looks us in the eye, swears he isn't using ANYTHING, and insists we have to accept what he says. And, oh yes, he'll do the suspension because they have no right to invade his privacy with U.A.s and we can't make him. And how can we? He's a six-foot-five, 215 pound, varsity defensive tackle and not a little kid any more. What options do we have? Throw him out? A minor? Emancipate him? We can't chain him to his bed; we can't spank or strong arm him. He no longer obeys anyone. He is different, and yet he *swears* he's not using.

Saw another battle-worn parent on a terrain walk. Her teenage daughter has run away again. Her summer of hell has turned into a winter's nightmare. All I say is, "I'm so sorry," and try to offer hope. Our older son, Jason, drove us crazy too, for a while—not as bad but he had some rough roads. Now he's attending college, just made the Dean's list and he's the one with ADD. They all get better someday. Don't they?

Joshua has to get through the next three and a half months of school without truancy. If it happens again, he's *expelled*. Unbelievable. The news drives nails into my brain. Addiction is a greedy disease. It snatches futures from young and old.

I stop at the mall to buy a couple of shirts on sale. I've just had lunch with two friends—when I run into Joshua.

I smile, tickled to get to see him unexpectedly, but when he approaches I read the signs. "Mom, I need to explain something." My heart drops along with contentment on my face. *Oh no, not again,* I think to myself, *not here, not in the glare of public scrutiny.* "What now?" I ask.

He was called into the school office. He and two kids were walking back after lunch from a friend's house. They had just entered campus territory when the other boys lit up cigarettes. Joshua says he told them, "Put `em out, you're gonna get caught," but they ignored him. Minutes later, two school security guards cruised by in a car and reported all three boys smoking. Joshua's argument is moving, rational, but nevertheless he's presented again with a two-week suspension. He swears to me he's innocent and I believe him.

Dropping my plans, I rush back to the car and rehearse my speech. Whereas I've avoided the school because of shame, now I'm a cold-blooded killer. I march into the principal's office: "Joshua is not perfect and has made mistakes but *this* time he's innocent!" I declare to the man in charge of his fate. "The other kids are willing to testify in his behalf," I go on with my argument. "Haven't you noticed a change in his behavior? When have you seen Joshua break down in tears? Hasn't he always taken his punishment like a man?"

"What credibility do kids have against two staff members, even though one took him aside and conceded she may have been mistaken? Anyone can make a mistake. It's easy to think you see three kids smoking when you know all have had tobacco violations in the past and you observe them from a moving vehicle. Clearly this is guilt by association. How many other times have parents appealed charges brought by these guards? And how does one measure bias and prejudice, much less visual acuity?"

Stopping at nothing to defend him, my mother- blood boils. Although I'm acting with respect, my assertiveness spikes with anger. The patronizing principal interjects, "Mrs. Garrison, you're raising your voice." I remain in control, although his punitive parent tugs at my inner child. He offers, "What if I lower the suspension from two weeks to one?" Incredulous, I exclaim, "Joshua shouldn't have to do a minute!" I reach out and touch his hand, "Please search your heart on this one."

We don't make waves or ask for favors. We face problems and hold Joshua accountable. But now he's trying and they seem to be lying in wait. Is this in society's best interest? Reputation is as fragile as a butterfly's wing. They think Joshua is a liar and a screw-up. They think I'm a histrionic nut. How they love to vilify the mother, demonize the child and protect the establishment. The principal asks if I think he is an advocate for students or staff. I say both, but silently I think he's an advocate for his own butt.

In hindsight, this was classic enabling. No doubt Joshua's credibility was damaged and I should have stayed out of the way. I never had the nerve to confront authority but just as the disease cripples, it can empower too, albeit in an enabling fashion. When I walked through those doors I was on fire with courage. Maternal ferocity increases as stakes are raised. It's a natural consequence when one foolishly squanders a reputation, people jump to conclusions. He wasn't smoking the cigarette…but he was a drug addict.

Tension stipples with a stiff brush. Bob sets up the appeal. I'm filled with dread and finish off a package of Mint Milano cookies. Suddenly, Joshua bursts through our front door and announces the principal persuaded him to settle out of court on an abbreviated suspension. Joshua acquiesces to get it over with and takes a freebie vacation with allowance for make-up work. Had he stopped to consider this was pretty much an admission of guilt, a third tobacco violation and a precedent to set him up for a more severe punishment? Like ninety days or expulsion?

I'm confused. Two weeks ago he was in tears declaring the fight of his life and now, although not admitting guilt, willing to take an unjust suspension. Why did I go to bat for him? He's at their mercy. He says the principal is his ally. How naïve.

We warned Joshua of an informal caucus. I hate defeat, especially when we're falsely accused. Joshua concedes he set himself up and thinks it's in his best interest to keep the principal happy. I will support his decision but I don't have to like it. I wonder where this animosity originates—I was a perfect kid in school. What unfinished business does this conjure? Oh, of course, it must be my dad issues.

What have I learned? Let your kids fight their own battles. Note how I so closely identified with Joshua, referring to "we" in the sentence, "falsely accused." I was unable to detach in a healthy way. His defeats became mine.

The following weeks bring more phone calls, anonymous and urgent. Call after call: rumors and ruminations shift us from good to awful parents. Only miserable failures raise addicts. Isn't that what the world believes?

Wretched and despondent, we're swirled into an eddy where hope cannot penetrate. How do you get back? How do you feel safe again? We're convinced Joshua's an addict; therefore deny him use of the car. We must protect ourselves and others. But this may mean a shutdown on his part. So far this quarter he's doing better in school. That could blow up but we have no other choice. Better to risk his education than to let him continue. The sooner he feels discomfort the sooner he may come out of denial. He won't get the privileges back until he goes into treatment, but first we need the U.A. and when you open that box the screamin' gremlins come flying out. Joshua breaks curfew and we walk the floor with fears too awful to imagine. Addiction is the

Bermuda Triangle of all diseases. Families disappear without a trace. They're either picked off one by one or sucked under as a unit never to be heard from again.

It's back to school after spring break. We've taken the car away, put a "For Sale" sign on it, and have stopped all money including lunch dollars. He'll have to brown-bag or go without. I've joined a support group called Al-Anon and the meetings comfort and empower. It's a shame-free zone and safe haven where you can be yourself. People understand before you open your mouth.

This morning I wait and brace for Joshua's reaction to the car sale. Expecting anything from compliance to rage, I'm relieved when the outcome is peaceful. He goes to school, takes a sack lunch, calls to check in and comes home on time. I approach to pat him on the back. Don't get me wrong—I'm not the least bit lulled into a false sense of security. We take things minute by minute. He's upstairs, doing homework and still denying he has a drug problem. He's volatile and at any time can do a 180-degree turn. We tiptoe, set limits and wait to see if he'll comply. We don't want him to run, so we do this dance.

I climb the stairs to check on him; he growls and tells me to close the door and flashes me a hateful look. Is he resuming homework or flipping me off? He's now on our house arrest and resenting every minute. As his anger increases do we hedge or pad our bets? Can we squeeze him into our demands? It's all uncharted territory. We feel our way in the dark.

Meth is the alpha male of monsters. Competing for dominance, it creates a tangled world where change favors the clever. Adapting, one must bend to survive or splinter into extinction. We sold the Subaru today with Joshua's CD player in it. We'll pay tomorrow. He'll punish us somehow, some way. Sure enough, the next day there's no check-in call and he doesn't come home until 10:00 P.M. I finally burst

11

into tears when he goes to bed.

The next morning, still punchy, I make a request, "Joshua, I'll pick you up after school so you can get your homework done. Please be there."

"Why should I do anything for you?" he snarls.

"Because I love you." I wonder how bad it will be tonight when Bob and I confront him but wave the thought away because I have to get to work. As he goes upstairs, I ask if he can bring the laundry basket down. I say it politely, but he barks, "Talk in a regular voice! I know that voice!"

Addiction peppers families with pocks of pain. But such an actress I am. I could rival all the greats with performances so real, so believable, not a person alive would suspect our happy little family is a fraud. I draw people out but carefully guard our secret and hide in plain sight.

Although both boys turn heads like their parents, the tall package looks good but belies the eye. Like smoke and mirrors, I take refuge behind the mask thinking it's better to isolate than risk the threat of exposure or glaring comparisons. I admire a friend, another parent of an addict. A nice stranger asks her in a store, "How are you today?" Without hesitation she answers honestly, "I feel like throwing a canned ham through a plate glass window."

* * *

We sleep fitfully for a week before confronting Joshua with the urine test. We pray he tests clean; therefore we wait in that special place called hope and shadows.

Monday morning comes and Bob readies himself. He will do the U.A. with Joshua's first morning pee. Joshua must take the U.A. or we will emancipate him. I pace like a cat anticipates an earthquake. I hope he won't balk, and better yet the results will be clean. You see, Friday night scared me. He talked way too fast and too much.

"Joshua, we're doing a U.A.," Bob announces.

"NAW!" "NAW!" "NO WAY!" he yells.

Bob makes a calm request and then another and another. The fear shakes me from the quiet place I go when terrified. *Oh God, he really is an addict.* Pleading, crying, threats and logic fall on deaf ears when your child is in the clutches of addiction. He sees your lips move but cannot hear a word you say. His brain is high jacked on a high-speed transport whizzing away at sonic speed. It propels, accelerates and catapults you into the abyss. A crooked finger holds on to the rim and turns bluish-white against the weight of our entire futures. Our baby, what can we do? The choices are both imminent and awful. Remain in denial and watch him kill himself or create a bottom for him this minute, this very second. Parents in pain, allowed to run loose, vanish over rims.

We make him an ultimatum and know we mean it. The risk is enormous. Here it is three weeks until the end of his junior year and he trains tomorrow for his summer job. He's attending school and passing classes, and yet we have to assign him the essential suffering.

Once I absorb the reality, I'm determined to drive a stake through the devil. We are risking his graduation, his job, the fact we may never see him again—everything to force a crisis. Sooner or later the crisis would come of its own, but when you're dealing with a deadly disease, sooner can mean the difference between life and death. He says he'll never take the U.A. and leaves, slamming the front door.

Later the same day:

Joshua just called and wants to know if he can come home. Says he'll take the U.A. but won't go to treatment. We tell him no, he can never come back unless he's ready, really ready to get well. He says he'll never go to rehab, "Cause they don't do crap." He'll call tomorrow. I say, "Fine."

That evening Joshua comes home; says he's willing to take the U.A. He probably drank a quart of vinegar to mask the results; he isn't motivated to stop only to regain the losses incurred. We let him stay figuring it's a move in the right direction. He reluctantly takes the U.A. although I'm sure it will test clean for crank because it's been too long. What a shame. We need proof positive. Joshua needs to know we know for sure.

The next morning he misses his school bus and I blow up. The venom spews with surprising and shocking vengeance. You can beat good dogs and usually they'll roll over and beg. But sometimes, they'll rise up and tear your throat open.

I was my mother's greatest joy, not heartache. My smoldering rancor's become more virulent. Have you turned your feelings off or pushed them down—so far down, they are expressed only in behaviors? What keeps us going? We drag ourselves together, trudge to work, eyes vacant and swollen. We do the laundry, fix the meals and hold our breath. It takes an altered state to get through it. Parents are pack mules, beasts of burden.

Has life knocked you down and asked you to play in spite of being hurt? You've suited up and turned out but sit on the bench? Does your coach, your Higher Power, ask the impossible—to keep giving your all when there are only seconds on the clock and you're so far behind there's no chance of ever catching up? No amount of chalk talk, pep talk or walking the walk can pin that win on your chest. You can't cross the finish line when your face is in the mud.

Chronic grief is solitary confinement; I like to think of stabbing it out of me. Although my rage is external, I turn it inward and feel it come up like a bad meal. This has been a tough day. Joshua lashes out and says, "What's your problem?"

"Sad. Do you have homework? If so, you need to do a half-hour."

"No! I have plans. You're so negative. I've learned all about positive and negative role models and you're a negative role model," he says, ripping me like a box cutter. Such viciousness I've never seen in him. Such abuse I will not tolerate. I crawl to bed for another cry and later tell him how mean it is to kick someone when they're already down. And no, I wouldn't have a couple of extra dollars, not when he talks to me like that. A half-ass apology followed, but you know, I stopped loving him a little more today.

I exist near the margins where dark things scurry in the corners. In the middle of the moment my cousin calls. I am a fine actress. I change the inflection and tone of my voice. Privacy has always been sacred and that helps justify the secret but like a Bukowski poem walking through fire, I do all I can to isolate but sometimes they slip through. Nothing is so telling as the not telling.

*   *   *

How did it come to this, my baby so estranged, so deranged? We give him the ultimatum: Go into treatment or move out. He chooses to leave. Is this a leap of faith or a desperate jump? Is it both? What if we're sentencing him to an earlier rather than later death? What if it backfires and his bottom is our abyss too?

Prayer is portable pain displacement, my anti-monster defense system. It bolsters courage to disclose to old friends but still not immediate family or local friends. That will come later when I'm strong or have no other choice.

I cloak myself in the ruse because I'm not prepared to reveal everything to everyone. We are as sick as our secrets. But as we grow and heal, we master boundaries and learn to say what we mean and mean what we say. This barefoot pursuit demands we create a bottom and simultaneously hit the wall. Joshua will go into treatment immediately or get

15

out. He's gone for a week and calls us in the middle of the night agreeing to our mandate. Of course the in-patient clinic is booked and we are on a waiting list but Joshua stays home to detox. All looks okay. He's in an anger control class and has cooperated with two U.A.'s. So why do I feel something terrible is about to happen?

His last U.A. was clean—great—but also no great surprise. Yesterday's U.A. no doubt will be too. But we're going to require he get another today and God only knows how he'll react. We talked to his counselor and concur it would have been perfect timing for Joshua to use yesterday, giving him several days before the next expected U.A. This will come as a shock—we're not as dumb as he thinks. But if he's clean we must bring up the subject, oh, so delicately. He's a powder keg ready to blow. If he's dirty, he'll throw a fit and we're back to square one. Crazy, crazy, we're ten on the crazy meter. Fear hovers like an icy ghost.

*   *   *

Today's the day Joshua was supposed to go into rehab but he passed the U.A. Lots of mixed feelings—relief but also dread if we are postponing the inevitable.

Tedium ad- nauseam: The next week I feel something isn't right, so ask Joshua if he's been drinking. He looks me in the eye and says, "No." I ask to smell his breath and sure enough he's been drinking. I'm numb and filled with white-hot rage. I collect my thoughts and shoot him a nasty look. His days are numbered. Each time you walk away with less hope. The rise and fall of promises wears us out. Each time you think, this is life and death. We have a bed date for him; he's going in-patient.

ESCAPE HATCH
August 23, 1997

KARLA KLEAR SKY enters the healing hut and sits cross-legged on the clay floor. She waits and beats her drum, beckoning the Great Spirit to fill her hurting heart and anoint the healing balm. She moans and hums her soul song as three tears descend her cheek. Her breath keeps cadence with the universe as her throbbing mind awaits the wisdom to be seen.

We return home from taking Joshua to rehab, a warren of wounded souls. A beautiful, tranquil place, set in a lush meadow surrounded by green grass and greenhorn parents, full of fear, doubt and desperate hope. Families from all walks of life—CEO fathers and mothers in designer clothes; middle-class moms and dads in jeans and cutoffs; one mother, skin and bones, tattoos exposed in revealing too-tight clothes, a house-arrest GPS leg band on her ankle, an endless parade of human wreckage, but parents, all hurting, all searching for the elusive something that can save their babies and keep them alive one more day.

Parents are trampled in the stampede to explain their children's addictions. Automatically defiled in a hierarchy of shame, they search for answers. Kids are hustled to dormitories where parents lick their wounds and wait for recovery that grants absolution.

It seemed our family landscape changed with the arrival of this monster. But the truth is, it was re-visited, not a first encounter. Addiction was the thread that left its indelible imprint on our disease-dominated world.

Rehab exhausted, I'm drained but with new

awareness. Boot camp readies me to confront and set better limits with Joshua. Although there are a slew of things the addict can use to slide out of responsibility, the same goes for parents. Although we did not cause addiction, we helped prop it up over time. I learned I wasn't a bad mother but an imperfect one. I made mistakes but did the best I could. I threw myself whole-heartedly into parenting but fell short in many areas: I was idealistic, perfectionistic, naïve and plain stupid. But more importantly, I was the adult child of an alcoholic. I never fully appreciated how the disease hobbled me in my family of origin or how to take care of myself constructively. I was either overly dependent or alienated others due to an underlying fear of abandonment. It also became clear Bob was damaged from his alcoholic family that added to the mix.

I had a pattern of catastrophizing that was traced to early conditioning. Convinced I was scorched and singed beyond repair, martyrdom was worn proudly. My life was transformed into duplicate goals: avoiding pain or wallowing in it. Withdrawal was a knee-jerk reaction making it easy to isolate and become an accomplished loner. No doubt I chose counseling as a profession to work through and empower myself by helping others. I learned early on if you want to be seen, stand up; if you want to be heard, speak up, but the only safe thing was if you want to be liked, shut up...don't talk, don't trust, don't feel.

Having felt like I came from a lower caste family, my desire to be perfectly pedigreed sought ways to extinguish the shame. Oh, I knew I had come from a long line of nuts. Aunt Laura hid her false teeth for the hell of it and another aunt ate rotten bananas and lost most of her mind after several abortions and the cruel thumb of a tyrannical husband. And Uncle Doag, the charming prevaricator, swore he wasn't lying or a rattlesnake would bite him in the mouth and great-grandmother Goodman, six-feet tall with a mane of Jewish curls and a temper like a cornered wolverine, kept her lanky boys in line with a bullwhip and sewed two toes back on one of them when his brother chopped them off with a wood axe for spite. And there was funny and equally nutty Aunt Billy who hoarded food, shopped compulsively and wanted, at age eighty-one, a personalized license plate that said, "Fuck You." And Uncle Dillon wrote hot checks, Aunt Margie abandoned her baby to chase the arms of a worthless boyfriend and Uncle Pink supposedly died when he peed on an electric fence.

And then of course, there was my dad—an abusive, alcoholic womanizer with delusions of persecution and a body printed with tattoos. His legacy was boozing and beating my mom and legally changing his name a half-dozen times. His birth name was Norman Lee Gilbreath but he changed that when he got mad at his alcoholic father, who reneged on a promise to let him have the money from the sale of a calf. The first name change was Norman Lee Hienz (pronounced like the ketchup, but misspelled because he wanted to be unique). That prank resulted in my birth name I defended to others my entire unmarried life, when people argued my name was either misspelled or mispronounced. How could I tell them my dad was a nut and it was all a farce anyway? Then he decided after my parents divorced he'd start anew and changed his name to Nick Lee Hienz…then Nick Hienz, then Nikkos Hienz, then Nikkos Leo Nidas and then Nick Leonidas. It was around the fourth change I wrote a seventeen-page letter saying I was disowning him as my father and also added he didn't have a drop of Greek blood and he could change his name to Onassis but it wouldn't make a bit of difference (as well as some other stuffed resentments).

Twenty-four years passed without a word and then shortly before he died I heard from his brother. I sent my father a kind letter and some pictures and wished him an easy death. I felt nothing then and feel nothing now. The opposite of love isn't hate…it's indifference. He was a hard-working, meticulous, ambitious man, but also a selfish, self-serving, violent, alcoholic nut. I never had a father but married Bob, who became not only the love of my life but the daddy I never knew.

Yes, at rehab we discovered and uncovered. My people came from Texas and spanned the social gamut from simple poor folk to the rich and haughty, from the healthy and mentally stable to sick alcoholic misfits. But deeply sewn into my soul was the awareness I was from a colorful but flawed stock, and that lineage, as someone described, helped shape my deformities.

With an earlier rupture of self and esteem, the legacy lingered. I thought an education could help me ascend the ladder out of disgrace. The family conjoint sessions were like a "SMACK," referring to a new cadet at West Point (Soldier Minus Ability, Co-ordination and Knowledge) and grueling tests of mettle where egos are detonated and new ones built in place. It was there I first examined the various barriers I had erected and recognized too, just because it's history, doesn't mean it's all in the past.

Having refused to look at my role as hero in my family of origin, I was equally reluctant to look honestly at my part in my primary home or I would swing far out and blame myself for everything. The irony was the more I hid my true self due to feelings of inadequacy and fear, the more I damaged my already fragile and broken self. Solitary and circumspect, I was cautious and prudent. I harbored animosity when I could not control the boys. As a child I was obedient because-

"That was a long time ago. In those days we did what we were told." —Ninety-one year-old woman speaking of her youth.

Similar to the matron in the above passage, I did what

was commanded without question or rebellion. I was intimidated by authority and easily manipulated by my children. I was emotionally volatile, a screaming maniac at times or serene and docile. I spanked, then stopped spanking—yelled and tried to reason. I bargained and bribed, fell apart and became a tyrant. I loved and nurtured and vilified, too. I made the usual mistakes and the unusual. I pleaded, guided, modeled and chided, taught and screwed up with the best but never sank as low as the worst. Yet, I loved my babies. I devoted body and soul to them and tried, tried to raise loving, decent human beings.

We learned in rehab, addiction is a disease of ironic contradictions. Although it cannot be cured, it can be managed. This flew in the face of previously held notions. Like other pundits, we argued it was not a disease but a self-serving choice; the answer was maturity born of humility. But it is a disease, not a choice. However, humility is a key to arresting the monster.

We also learned if Joshua didn't stop drinking, the alcohol would turn his liver into a cyst- filled, fatty blob that would shut down and kill him. And if he didn't stop the other drugs, he would have permanent brain damage and an equally early demise. But in addition, alcoholics-addict's brains are different from the start. Alcoholics get up to ten times the reward from alcohol as social drinkers because addiction is a genetic pleasure-pain disorder. First they drink and drug to feel good, then they drink and drug to stop feeling bad.

With that first day at rehab our odyssey began. Laser-focused to pound addiction into remission, I had more passion than direction but knew instinctively this thing was out to kill us, part and parcel. With that agenda I hit the ground running. I would not only fix Joshua but I would do it full throttle. Who wouldn't jump into a frozen lake to save their child?

Nevertheless, I'm tearful and confused. Joshua is safe in treatment and yet I live in the unknown. Why can't I stay in the here and now? Things heard at rehab: "Teeth knocked out and raped repeatedly," quicken my pulse and deepen my dread. Definition of a mother? Full contact misery. Every four hours an addict takes his or her life. Every two hours an addict is murdered. Every four minutes one dies of an overdose.

* * *

I notified Joshua's school he'd be late starting his senior year. Such sadness, it cuts into hearts and carves souls to pieces. When you love children, you hold them in a special place that's impenetrable. It's baffling, the pain is immense and yet the love remains. When you love children, you are forever bonded.

Someone spoke about a forest fire in Yellowstone National Park, when rangers found a petrified bird perched on the ground like an inanimate object. Knocking it over, three tiny chicks scurried out from under their dead mother's wings. She had instinctively known to protect them from the toxic fumes and scorching heat. She could have flown to safety but she was a mother and her love compelled her to stay until the end.

* * *

Four weeks pass and Joshua gets out of treatment. I approach his dorm with trepidation. Has it worked? I open the corridor door to see Joshua's counselor in the hall. I smile but the greeting is not returned. Is he preoccupied with something? It seems so, there's no clue the seriousness of his demeanor is due to Joshua. I test the waters, "Well, he finally made it," I try to say cheerfully. But the therapist's expression tells me otherwise as he ushers me into a room with four somber counselors, two I've never met.

I see Joshua sobbing, red-faced and slumped in a chair. My knees buckle hearing the rehab director's words,

"Joshua violated the no-female rule last night and horse-played in his room. His treatment will be deemed, not completed." I'm too numb to speak—too shocked, too sad and overwhelmed to do or say anything. Slack-jawed, I sit like a clump of cream of wheat, white and silent. Joshua defends himself, explaining he misread cues that the last night was forgiving. He struggles to speak through gasps as tears flow from his blue eyes. He's sorry and apologetic—thinks I'm angry and I counter, "Not angry but disappointed," stressing rules must be followed. Some back and forth statements and all is over in a speckled moment.

Thinning the herd. Why can't anyone have something nice to say about my son? Was this so terrible a crime? Enabling is the buzzword for defending them. Isn't it setting kids up by mixing and then requiring them not to form relationships? Why not have a keg in the snack room and instruct them not to look or go near *it*?

I'm too tired to fight. I leave the room with their sad eyes and indelible pity —the way it is when they lead you to that other austere corner in a hospital and prepare you for your loved one's death.

Could they be wrong? Oh, dear God, please let them be wrong. I want to be with Mom. She would hold me and tell me it's not my fault; she would comfort and listen and sit with me when I wake in the night. Oh Mom, our lives are a shambles. I don't know how to feel happy or trust. How can we save him? Blues is a good parent feeling bad. How do I dial heaven?

* * *

A week later and everything looks good when hope is hungry. Joshua wakes up easily and in a happy mood. He goes to church and lunch with us; smiles, converses and doesn't panic when I open his book-bag. He asks in a calm voice when he wants something and inquires about location and directions to A.A. meetings. He comes home before curfew and doesn't lose his temper or curse. His hygiene is meticulous and he sounds enthusiastic about his senior year. But as I'm leaving for a workshop, he gives me a warm hug and kiss asking sweetly for a half-hour extension on his curfew. Am I content to merrily agree to divert an argument—or am I just giddy from his charm?

It is a workshop on domestic violence prevention. I sit in a circle with a dozen people. The facilitator, a woman psychologist, asks each of us to introduce ourselves and briefly explain why we came to the training. As she nods to her right, signaling the first person to begin, a nice-looking lady on her other side asks politely if she can first pass around homemade cookies fresh from her oven. Smiling and accommodating, the doctor takes one of the cookies and passes the tray to the gentleman on her right, again asking him to start the introductions. Each person in turn shares their name, occupation and the reason for their attendance. Each takes a cookie and passes the platter around the circle— everyone except a policeman, who declines the offer.

Finally, when all have been introduced, it is the cookie lady's turn. She says her name and explains she isn't a professional but wants to learn how to avoid domestic violence because she and her husband have terrible arguments ever since she came under investigation for poisoning her boss!

Alarm falls over the group as faces drain of color and eyes dart with fear. But the policeman looks down, avoiding the temptation to gloat or call the rest of us idiots. According to a template, a prescribed course of expected behavior, all but one politely and eagerly took from that inviting plate. And as we munched the delicious cookies, we swallowed those morsels along with naiveté coming away full of fear but brimming with wisdom. Trust can be a synonym for stupidity. Joshua came home an hour late.

With increased surveillance, I ask Joshua how the

A.A. meeting went the next night. Although I tried and failed to locate the address to check on him, I sense he hasn't attended. He looks me in the eye and lies. It turns my stomach. Lies slide easily across his lips like cream from silver ladles. Checking up, following and questioning are classic co-dependent behaviors. My relapse and his are imminent.

Bob and I open the conversation but focus on confronting, not attacking, on feelings and objectives. Yes, he's serious about recovery but too busy, too tired to attend a meeting, needed a break, needed downtime— manipulations or revelations? We remember our choices; remember our boundaries. He will go to meetings and after-care, no excuses or exceptions. Is he already using, only sixteen days out of treatment?

A friend calls to complain about a minor problem and she has a life that is nearly perfect. Now wouldn't she have a tough time if she were worried sick about her child? My tolerance is low. Friends irritate like a wool blanket against sunburn. A critical attitude is a barrier to friendship.

Other bad signs: Joshua's late again for curfew. This time eighty-five minutes. Less interaction. Less conversation. Less eye contact. I fix lunch and grill cheese sandwiches on the griddle until golden brown. Then slice them into neat triangles and serve them with tomato soup and crackers. We bite in eagerly but are surprised and disappointed to find I have forgotten to put cheese between the bread. The disease distracts and hampers even simple pleasures.

The following day, I ask Joshua to mow the lawn. An argument starts and he agrees to do part of it. I compromise, figuring something is better than nothing. But later, when he's in the process of the chore, I realize I'm giving up my authority to him again. I demand he finish the job and threaten to kick him out. Funny, isn't it? This same day of the first substantial argument since his return from rehab, he came up hot for pot. I was wrong changing demands midstream and controlling him with threats, but he was already toxic…again.

*   *   *

The next morning we announce, "Joshua, it's time for another U.A." Immediately an argument erupts. Bob threatens, "Pack your shit if you won't comply." I break down in tears. I sense Joshua, with his cocky, distant smugness is relapsing. He won't let me hug him and that's always using evidence. Warnings flash the fear. We wake in the night and find him missing.

The next day we go to Al-Anon and discuss serenity. What a challenge to achieve peace. Now I understand the counselor's eyes. They had seen it all too often these unscheduled departures. Their sadness and compassion fastened with pity and knowledge. They knew the journey upon which we were about to embark. They knew Joshua was a moment's breath from relapse.

Working without a net, we strive for homeostasis—to fix, control and cure the incurable. This hyper-vigilance squeezes everything with the focus collapsing and our family going down for the third count. But just when we think we have descended into hell, Joshua begs us to take him back. Because we love him and have been told relapse is part of recovery, in fact 92% of meth addicts relapse, we agree to let him try again.

Last night we went to church. Joshua said he was getting a ride with a friend but wasn't there when we arrived. Later, when we walk into our family room to face the crisis, Joshua confesses he's relapsed on shrooms and is having a bad trip. Agitated and restless, he taps a foot and checks the clock a dozen times while rubbing sweaty hands back and forth on shaky thighs. Terrified of 9:11, he says, "It's an ominous sign." I try to comfort and remind him it's only drug- induced paranoia. He presents as remorseful and appears newly motivated but I have doubts and countless fears. If we turn him out, our greatest worry is suicide, which he threatens all the time.

*   *   *

The next weekend, Joshua calls and says he needs a ride home. His friend ditched him and he knew he'd be in trouble if he were late. "Oh yes, you would be so gone," I say, impressed by certainty in my voice.

Is that why I invited everyone for Thanksgiving? Anger empowers. We do not deserve, nor will we tolerate one more broken curfew. I will ride into that sunset, head cocked back and the wind in my hair. Good news about other children will leave warmth in my heart—not sobs so great it wracks and heaves.

We have to be out of town in preparation for Jason's wedding. When we need the most serenity, Joshua's disease rears its ugliness. No check-in call and terror closes its fist. There goes the ceremony and there goes our cover. If we put him out we'll have to reveal the secret. Not here. Not now. Not in the midst of the wedding. But he's unreliable—we'll have to have a back-up best man just in case.

I long for a good night's sleep. I cancelled Thanksgiving; had to call out-of-town and out-of-state guests who had already purchased airline tickets. Local friends, as well, are disappointed and maybe angry, too. But I just can't pull it off, although for a brief moment I thought I could have a normal life.

With a rising chorus of doubts our resolve crumbles as he begs and pleads for another chance. He swears he's not drinking (we know he's not drugging because we test) arguing he's doing well in school. "PLEASE, PLEASE, can't you be patient?" he asks tearfully. We cave in again and hope we can get through the wedding and the rest of his senior year. But another missed curfew and we make him leave Friday night. We'll have to use the back-up best man and the secret will be out. But what can we do? He refuses to return to rehab and at eighteen we can't force him.

Sunday night sets into action the latest crisis: Joshua drives drunk, totals a car and does four days in jail. We suffer as our lives spin out of control. The first phone call says he's in the accident, then a second call from someone reporting the passenger in the other car has been "seriously injured," which, thank God, isn't so.

Despondent, Joshua begs to come home but we are cold, detached and then full of self-doubt agonizing with our decision but refusing his request. Quickly we get to Al-Anon; lots of pros and cons on giving him another chance. One woman says her fifty-five year-old brother still runs to Mom for rescue. But another shares how parents turned their back on a son who later hung himself in their garden shed.

We let him come home. Now part of me is relieved to have him alive, safe within our refuge but another part is waiting for the next crisis. Oh God, please help him stay motivated. Please protect others from him. Please help us all. Toxic weight from toxic stress elevates cortisol, which taxes and compromises not only immune systems but spiritual defenses, too.

After soul-searching we agree school is a dangerous trigger. Joshua drops out his senior year and drops all friends, avoiding any place where he's tempted to relapse. Although this breaks our hearts, it feels like the right decision. He is clean, sober, serious and appears greatly changed by the car wreck. This Saturday he will take his GED test. He has a good job, is going to A.A. meetings and will start college next quarter. We're going to counseling, Al-Anon and for now things are improving. I disclose to local friends and out-of-state relatives. This is excruciating but we ride a nice wave for a couple of weeks. This short respite is better than most because I feel better prepared for what may, probably will come. Al-Anon is my parent-protection program.

Joshua gets his GED and is gone most every day working. The peace and quiet is welcome. Things seem different because things are different—no school, friends or drugs. I prayed God would send us something or someone who would be a conduit for change. The answer for us was the coalition of Al-Anon. The group attenuates the disease, allowing movement both in and out of crisis more rapidly. This transition from survival to living is an important first step. Why the rousing endorsement? Because no one judges. Parents are at the forefront and always implicated when kids are involved with alcohol and drugs. It's not fair or proven. I'm reminded what Miami Herald syndicated columnist and father of five, Leonard Pitts Jr., Pulitzer Prize winner says, "Parents can't make their child someone he is not."

Al-Anon pulls me from the wreckage. When severely depressed I couldn't take action, but empowered now, I'm putting myself together. I'm learning I can't fix him but I can fix *me*. I can't always get what I want but I can get over what I can't have. But fears are canyon walls that stretch like gray solemn giants holding up the sky as we paddle into the gorge and make our way across cold, deep water. Blowflies bite and pester, but we swat them and good sense away ignoring every warning.

Karla Klear Sky

30

TWO

Monsters & Madness

1998

Addiction robs life in steady increments, which result in unrivaled extortion. In spite of antabuse, Joshua relapses the night of Jason's wedding. Hotel security wakes us at three o'clock in the morning reporting he is screaming and out of control. Warning they are about to call the police, Bob placates the staff, but I'm sick with fear. We open the door to Joshua's room where we find him on the floor, semi-conscious, in a puddle of vomit with the sour stench of spilled booze and distilled dreams. I stay up with him the rest of the night with his head cradled in my lap, checking his pulse and staring into darkness.

Sunday morning we pile into cars, say our goodbyes to family and friends, unaware of the previous night, hug, kiss and force smiles on our plastic faces. We drive four hours taking guests to the airport, counting the minutes until we collapse and retreat to our holes.

Now it's been three days with little sleep. Joshua remembers nothing since he was in a blackout—says he's sorry. Yeah. The disease teaches us never to count on anything.

In a single week's sad span, Joshua goes to court for the DUI and is now on a two-year probation. He's dropped off the following evening drunk. Should we throw him out or make him our prisoner? Suicide threats hold us hostage.

How do we drag ourselves along this entrenchment? Life is easy when the kids are great. But what if your child has a deadly disease with a single-minded purpose to kill the host and the family near and dear to it?

As we repel into the unknown, things get worse. I don't know what keeps me going. I want to discuss it and process with Bob but he is distant. I feel alone and discouraged. The free-range beast pounces again and knocks me into a new depression. We're all sick from this contagion. Or as someone said, "We're ordinary people surviving extraordinary pressures."

Days pass and Joshua's on the brink of something big and bad. He's struggling with boredom. I hope he can enlarge his social circle within the confines of recovery, but fears return and sleep is broken. My forecasting is prescient. On some level, I know or have knowledge of things before they happen. And sure enough the sluice swamps us again. Joshua calls his boss to take a float day in order to insure a longer night out, which will also free up time for make-up sleep. I'm disgusted —he does this minutes before work closes so we can't demand he call back. He may or may not have planned this, but I disrespect him all the same.

Bob disgusts me too—he's so passive I want to puke. I will have to set boundaries again and look like the heavy. I'm in a blue funk allowing Joshua's decisions to color affect. The train is coming and all I can do is jump out of the way. Bob's even stopped trying, which creates more frustration. Joshua rationalizes and Bob minimizes and I want to scream. Best described by someone else, "We're under the influence that ripens rage and orders disobedience."

Nasty, like a rat's breath, more and more tension, arguments, yelling and hard feelings. It twists me into tighter knots. Joshua rides his bike to class and works out at the gym. I agree to pick him up but take a nap and I'm late. I apologize but as we head home he complains, "I need to drive—I can't do this—I need a car!" I'm tired and don't want to fight but he keeps on and on. I explain he doesn't have enough clean/sober time to justify driving. He argues, "I'm the best of anyone! You just want to piss me off. What are you going to do, kick me out if I don't kiss your ass?" "Yes," I say, "If life is a war zone, I *will* kick you out." I'm sick of the bickering. When we get home I go upstairs to cry and take a time out. Later that evening, he knocks on the door and announces he's getting a ride to counseling. How can I agree to put him behind a wheel? He hates me because I won't give him what he wants. I hate him for demanding what I cannot morally give.

Burnout is a gap between effort and reward. Joshua relapses and breaks curfew again. He's dropped off on the front porch in a stupor, so out of it he can barely walk. He stumbles and falls on the living room floor where we leave him till morning.

Disorder is the genesis of depression. It holds thick, although there's a heart's desire for promises and remorse. Even if promises were empty, they would be welcome instead of wary acknowledgments, cool distancing and blank reptilian stares. Is it a hangover, or is there more in that stranger's face?

Resentment scrapes my mood. The next day Joshua wants a ride to class but I refuse. He walks to the bus stop and misses it by seconds, probably on purpose. He calls asking for a ride. I should let him squirm. Nonetheless, I pick him up, but to his surprise drop him off halfway there. By the look on my face, he knows I'm in no mood for an argument. Focused like a falcon, my eyes warn, *I'm all used up.*

That evening the phone rings; its Jason calling from the fitness center where his brother works. "I have bad news," he says with that familiar fear in his voice. My first words, "Is Joshua at the gym?" "No Mom, he no longer works here." Worry washes over me. Jason has no other information, and even if he did, like a leap off the center span of the Narrows Bridge and a drop into eight-knot reverse currents, back eddies make baffles next to useless.

By the time Jason and his wife arrive, we still haven't heard from Joshua. A delivery boy with fried chicken rings the doorbell. He's a former druggie friend of Joshua's who's managed to hold school, job and sports together in spite of alcohol/drug abuse...*abuse* not addiction. Every bite of dinner is wasted on jitters and jumbled thoughts. I want to shriek and fall to the floor, writhe in pain, tug at my clothes, pull out my eyelashes and mess in my pants. I want to scream and gasp and expel the fear. I want the world to know right here, right now, our son's in imminent danger.

It's official, Joshua's been fired from *another* job, again an alcohol-related dismissal. The worst part is his lack of remorse, and then off jokin' and smokin'. My rage whirls me loose wanting to destroy everything in my path. I hate everyone and everything and mostly him. My thoughts are murderous and savage. He threatens suicide; I counter, "Who should be more tempted?" Year after year living from crisis to crisis; life still disappoints with regularity. I called him a loser and a baby today. I must learn to hold my tongue. I'm sure I made it worse. Did I enjoy it, too?

Furious, but fortified, more frogs fall from the sky. Joshua doesn't come home again. I creep into bed, fourth try, around 3:00 A.M. Bob is also awake and trembling. We hold hands in silence and somehow give way to exhaustion and fall asleep in each other's arms.

I'm ashamed for calling Joshua a loser. I know it's destructive and yet I choose to abuse. The battle is fear and doubt. My world has so often been a scary place. If I can predict disaster, I can defend myself, although it's hard to prepare for something you know might kill you.

Thank God there is a message on the machine from a girl we don't know, relaying to us about you- know- who. He's okay, not in jail and will contact us later. As night falls so does optimism. I'm shaky—dropping things, spilling and tripping. Never can relax—never, ever. Fear dangles like a spider. Although he's in acute peril, there's nothing from Joshua and nothingness from me. It's astonishing; like Monet at the end of his life, "I no longer feel anything."

Another week and still no contact from Joshua; the fear grows thick and steady with ruminations numerous and powerful. I repeat to myself, *Karla, never ever part with harsh words.* Please, dear Lord, please let him be okay. If he is, he must be loaded, right? Because how could he forget to call me on Mother's Day? I know he loves me. I know he knows I love him. Please let him forgive me for proclaiming the future with bleak predictions. Please give me another chance.

Two more days and he's really hurt me this time. Please let him be safe. Please let him call today…eight hours later, he calls and he is okay. Thank you, Lord.

A Mothers' Day Card on Time, from Jason, our older son.

Eute, (nickname Jason calls me)   ***May 9, 1998, Mother's Day***
I just want to say how good a mother you have been to me and Joshua. Even if it feels at times you might have failed somewhere, that's only due to our poor choices. We know right from wrong; we always have. We just make stupid decisions at times and that's not your fault. We have better morals than most anyone I know, but teens will either choose to stick to `em or screw'em, and a parent can't be held responsible. I love you with all my heart and always will, and thanks, Mom, for molding me into a fine young man; try to forget my teenage years! I love you and thank you, Ranj (nickname I call Jason)

A late Mother's Day card from Joshua.

Mussie, (nickname Joshua calls me*)*   *May 14, 1998*

I have been a real punk and you don't deserve it at all. I guess it is just the period of time I am in right now. Mom, I love you a lot, and I understand why you are on my case all of the time. I just know teens and parents don't get along all that well, but it will be better in the future. Mom, I want you to know I really feel bad for all the wrong things I've done and I promise deep in my heart I never intended on hurting you. Remember I am your son Joshua, and I will always love and respect you. Happy Mothers Day & Love,   Josh

Joshua's been home four days and the friction is already building. The pitch, yaw and roll leave me conflicted. I love him, I hate him, I hate what our lives have become and he hates what he has become.

Joshua's note to himself.   *May 18, 1998*

I look at myself in the mirror and I call myself a puss. I can't believe its senior ball tonight. Why did I corrupt my life? I hate this disease. All my trouble revolves around my disease. I never mean to hurt anybody! But I need to watch for my decision making on self-destructive activities because that hurts others. Sad night. I'll try to think, but escaping seems easier.

Joshua relapses again.

Watch my heart explode like it's filled with nitroglycerin completely unaware of that nebulous abyss you're in. You flounder near the boundaries, while groping for your eyes, and mourn the fact your thoughtless act gave blindness as the prize.

An anonymous addict

We make Joshua move out again at eighteen and release him on his own recognizance. We're not sleeping. Fears flay us with incessant worries. We find him a modest apartment, all utilities paid and a maintenance job in the same complex. The reality sets in and he's scared. We're scared too, and incredibly sad it's come to this. But we have a clear conscience and pray he can make it. Of course the odds are heavily against that. He's still using, in denial and not ready to work a program. How long before he's re-arrested, evicted or both? How long before he overdoses and dies?

We have done much wrong—too permissive and passive at times, hard and hysterical at others. But I'm letting go of the regrets —maybe the shame will dissipate too. Trying to put faith in God—not future trip when Joshua self-destructs and turns into a homeless indigent. I'm off-balance and tearful, preparing for the worst and hoping for the best. But it's already nice having the house to us—tranquil rooms, quiet nights and phones that rarely ring.

Still tremendous grief as graduation approaches. Although Joshua won't graduate, hopefully we have to permanent empty nesters and post-graduate co-dependents. A decorated high-school senior's car sits next door urging me to look. Terrible imaginings beckon me into the pit. Worse case scenarios storm my mind as old torments beat their drum… this will never be over, be over, be over.

But life-altering events come unexpectedly. Without planning, I decide to pull into Joshua's apartment complex on my way home from work. Hoping he would be busy with his maintenance job, I'd just say a quick hello. But when he's nowhere around, at first disappointment is quickly tempered with a kind of expectance: he overslept, quit or has been fired *already*.

On shaky legs I climb the stairs to his apartment. Should I turn and run? No response to my knock, although the radio is blaring. I try the knob and sure enough, the door's unlocked. Tentatively, I push it open a tiny bit and peek in. I call his name through the small crack when a blast of tobacco smoke makes me recoil. Just then he appears from around the corner looking sleepy, startled, loaded and convicted. I begin the debate but his lame excuses are a poor challenge. He is defenseless and has nothing to say.

I walk away permanently altered. I found Joshua in his apartment loaded when he should have been at work, but I also found myself. What was the culmination of years took place in five minutes—no yelling, tears or pleas. While driving home, it all became transparently clear: Joshua's a *real* addict and this is what they do. I can continue with unrealistic expectations or accept what I cannot change. Spotting truth is tough. How can you tell an addict's lying? Their lips are moving.

*   *   *

Now open for business, Bob and I go to a softball game followed by a pizza party. Trying to connect with the world, we find we're painfully out of practice but tiptoeing back...waking at three to pee, not panic. But the debt-collector robs the progress. Poised and waiting the next day is a neighbor's invitation to their child's graduation party from high school.

When it's in your face, it's hard to look away. Our son has not, will not and did not graduate. How I despise this disease that transformed this child. Nothing can ever rectify, compensate or repair this utter loss, this falling away of dreams. We moan, but no one hears our whimper. We look normal and yet we have been mortally wounded. This is the circle of hell we created: the monster tosses lives and scatters souls like snow drifts stacked in shadows. Harvest time—what the monster gets, the monster keeps.

The following week, Joshua sees me gather the last of his clean laundry; gives me a big hug and says, "Mom, I really love you, I really do." I want to beg and lecture but stop and hug him hard. I'd rather have Joshua's genuine love than diploma and cold contempt, as some children have for their parents. Clean and sober, loaded or depraved, I know my boy truly loves me and as he so often says, he never means to hurt us.

* * *

I'm angry at a friend but my pattern is to stuff and act out pain. Consequently, we have both said hurtful things, but I excuse myself because she threw the first barb. We're trying to get past it but hard feelings linger. My guard is up. How can I trust her? It took courage to confront and share inner pain, only to be judged and condemned. She doesn't care; especially if it scuffs her day. You can be miserable but do it silently.

Exclusion and separation are kissing cousins of the monster. Bob and I won't go to her party. We can't sit through an evening with pseudo-friends who don't give a flying fig. Each loss multiplies exponentially. Forgiveness has always been difficult and now it's more pronounced. Bob, always forgiving by nature, also finds himself isolating. Submerged resentment rumbles in our gut; we can't plow the party with painted grins.

A LETTER NEVER SENT

Dear Friends and Family,   *June 1998*

Why haven't you written or called? Our child has a life-threatening disease and few ever ask—how he's doing or what it's like for us.

I know we don't call as often and cancel engagements, too. We brood and isolate, but could you understand better if he had leukemia and remissions that fail? Would you brag to a family about your child if they were battling a terminal illness? Or would you listen and not judge?

39

It's a long and lonely road to recovery. Please inquire—not pity but empathy is all we ask. I know you've had bad days too, but when bad days stretch into years it takes a toll. Why should something—anything work out when so much hasn't, time and again? With each crisis, life erodes until eventually it's a jagged cliff crumbling at one's feet and all we can do is back away from the precipice.

Remember, when people are unlovable, they need the most love. Each day we struggle with denial and delusion that tells our child he isn't sick but the world is, a disease that waxes and wanes and changes in an instant and we along with it. A disease that so preoccupies, we appear stupid when in fact we are overwhelmed with worry and sheer survival. A kind of low-grade fatigue envelops and disorients.

Like the time I was in Hawaii. I was staying at the military R & R center waiting for Bob to arrive from Viet Nam. Jet lagged and anxious, I fell into a deep sleep. As I napped, my body lurched and awakened. Dazed and confused, I startled, then panicked when I looked at my watch and it said 12 o'clock. "Oh my God, I've overslept and missed his plane!" Jumping to my feet I noticed a peculiar glow coming from the closed shutters. It was the afternoon sun, not moonlight squeezing through the slats...it was noon not midnight and several hours before his arrival. But in dogged grogginess for an instant I was sure it was night when it was day—sure of something and sure of nothing except the concussion of anxious exhaustion. And so it is with this disease.
We need your understanding and love.
Bob, Karla, Jason and Joshua

Survivors of addiction are similar to crime victims, and indeed, society associates addiction with crime. It is a crime to possess, use, sell, manufacture and distribute drugs.

In a utopia, illegal drugs would not exist; therefore addicts would turn to other things to satisfy their compulsions. But addiction is a result of biological forces supported and propelled by chemicals that alter minds.

This mega monster freezes faces, stunned and searching, then cuts out beating hearts and throws lifeless bodies down steep steps. But these instruments of torture deceive. Ever wonder who was hungry enough to pull that first thorny leaf from an artichoke and keep peeling until the succulent center was carved from the thistle? You can't know a kernel of truth until seeds grow into strong stalks.

Joshua saunters in like a pimp in a pink fedora. While loading his clothes in the washer, he says, "Love you, Mom." I reply, "I know but it changes nothing." I continue, "You're headed for prison as well as an early death." He shrugs and turns away. Forget the adage, "The apple doesn't fall far from the tree." Some apples fall from sturdy trees, perched high on hills with vertical slopes and very long rolls.

The next day I page him three times with no answer. I must stop doing this. My mind runs wild through bullet holes and dry blood. I wish I had left him with loving words.

Extended family is coming this weekend. I so wanted to avoid this but it looks like we will be forced to disclose or hide and sweat it out. God, please help us live through this one. I hurt for him. I hurt for all of us and every person affected by this ghoul.

More debris and ash disposal: The long friendship continues to unravel. I give up. The disease steals everything. I'm too tired and weary to defend the sanctimonious, dismissive sneers. I'm running on fumes and depleted from a lifetime of people-pleasing. I don't have the energy or inclination to work this hard. Débridement is another word for pulling off scabs, necessary, but disfiguring.

Joshua comes home again for a visit. He is friendly, loving and a little wistful about the "good old days" of living with the "P's" (Parents). Nice to see him; nice to see him go.

Worked through some differences with my friend but there is permanent damage. I'm growing however, because it no longer keeps me up at night. I will turn only to those who love me; who love me even when I'm unlovable.

I call Joshua —he's rushing to get another job. I hang up feeling hopeful he is doing something productive, only to have him ring the doorbell a couple of hours later. Horrible, unhealthy work—he just couldn't stand it and quit on the spot. He is ravenous and tearful as he gorges leftovers. All day I'm despondent. As school approaches I'm bracing for the anniversary response. This time last year we were looking at his in-patient treatment and senior year. All crumbs swept in a bin.

Joshua stops by again. He's jubilant in stark contrast to the day before. He has a remarkable ability to live in the moment, which I envy. Although he's facing jail, fines, poverty and God only knows what else, he doesn't dwell on it. I continue to fight old behaviors and am proud to announce I don't preach or help with the laundry or send him off with groceries. The pain is less and faith stronger but I'm still wary of my friend. I could move past this better if she really cared.

Another friend cancels lunch at the last minute. Her excuse: she needs a date with her husband. I'm disenchanted with the human race.

A few weeks pass and we find a note on our porch.

To my loving parents,   *August 31, 1998*
   I love you with all my heart. More than anything, I'm scared I am going to lose you and I don't think I would survive.
   Ever since I moved into this apartment, I have been using like crazy. I am an addict and have no control over

what I am doing. It is ruining me and taking me down. When I am high, I have no care and don't realize how much Satan is controlling me. I have come to my complete bottom and am getting terribly depressed and sometimes suicidal. What I would do to have this disease lifted from me. I have decided I have to get into reality and get happy again and bring up my serenity. My stealing and lying and cheating were not the way I was brought up and not the way I want to be deep down inside. I AM FREAKING OUT. I also am sober writing this. I am evicted from my apartment and am cleaning up with my roommate right now. I have a plan and I would like to talk to you about it.

With my money from work, when I find a job and go there every day, I am going to pay off my landlord completely. Then I am going to pay back all my debts. I will, I will, I will. I have a court date on September 15th and I will do everything they tell me and stick with it till the end! I know I am going to jail and am going to step up to the plate and face it. And if I have fines after, I will pay them, too. Mom and Dad, I don't like to be evil; I like to be good. I want my slate clean. It is not too late and I am going to prove it to myself and to you and God. When I die I want to die good with God. I am going to an A.A. meeting tonight. Not because someone's making me, but because I need to. I can't do it myself. I don't want to steal. I don't want to use. I have not been happy for months. I miss security; I miss love, happiness and light. I am so sick of living in the darkness. Please don't disown me. You're all I've got. I love and appreciate everything you've done for me with all my heart. I PROMISE I am going to "beat" it this time.

Love, your son, Joshua

Cranked high: Imagine every worry and bad memory eradicated in an instant. If you're weak, now suddenly strong; in mourning, quickly comforted; insecure, now confident; inept, recast as capable. A wallflower shifts, sexy and

43

appealing; once shy, now instantly charismatic. Imagine the bills all paid, responsibilities lifted and concerns melted away. Once fat, now thin; bald, now hair thick and full; old, now again young and vital; bored, immediately entranced; ordinary, suddenly made extraordinary! Imagine shame transmuted to pride; apart, now among; separated, now belonging; poor, now rich; sick, quickly healed; hurting, promptly soothed; guilty, now finally pardoned.

Picture dissatisfaction exchanged for content. Once lonely, now included; ravenous, suddenly satiated; lazy, now driven; exhausted, keenly energized! Envision lying manipulation swapped for clever resourcefulness. Once impotent, now virile! Imagine being uncomfortable in your own skin but reinvented whole and at one with the universe. Imagine everything ever imagined bathed in euphoric Technicolor. Once doomed, now set to soar on a comet's tail. Once defeated, now riding into the gates of Rome victorious! Imagine all this for the taking, readily at hand, instantaneous, all encompassing, all consuming. No responsibilities, no worries, fears, tears, debt, demands, commands, except the obsession and compulsion to recapture the apparition again, and again and again.

Best described by someone in recovery, "The disease makes addicts believe what they want to believe and go to the gallows with a smile on their face. It draws them down the passageway that pulls irresistibly to free, floating freedom …then closes in behind them. Trapped by the ice floe, they wait for the spring thaw that never comes, preventing their safe return."

Almost a year ago Joshua was midway through rehab and what progress has it brought? A high school drop-out, kicked out and now evicted and showing up on our porch. Of course we let him come in—until he goes to court, jail and rehab. He says all the right things but we're guarded too. He's a temporary guest and can be banished at any time.

This morning I write a beautiful card and leave it for Joshua by the bathroom sink. But an hour later I wake him and his stinging glance opens my anger. Joshua makes the point if I vacillate between support and hostility it will drive him out the door to use. Although I concede hostility is detrimental, he is still responsible for his sobriety.

My friend calls. I detect something in her voice. She wants another heart-to-heart veiled in contempt. But her tone softens when I mention the latest crisis. She wants details— not a chance. I no longer trust her and will censor carefully my disclosures.

Joshua's coming down from a long binge; he's grouchy and exhausted. The growling discourages efforts to connect. Post-active use creates the crank crash; extreme fatigue, depression and a ravenous appetite. He says he feels weak and over-whelmed. Don't we all?

Our options are limited: We won't pay fines, repay hot checks or write the eviction response. But should we let him stay? We are torn between imprisonment within our home or having to identify his body.

I stare out the window and see twins trot to kindergarten. My son, once full of promise, has come to this. I looked forward to uncovering his potential not the sheet over his face. Like a coroner's apron, life is stiff and stinking.

* * *

Short-term memory impairment intensifies during a crisis. I've hidden my wallet from Joshua and have searched for an hour and cannot find it. Frantic because I'm late for an appointment, I zigzag through rooms, wild-eyed with pulsing panic.

Later the same day resentment runs deep as the snapping sickness poisons all. Joshua's watering plants and the hose tangles on the hook; he throws it in disgust and walks away. Dripping sarcasm, I lob a crooked scowl and add, "Oh yes, just too much Joshua, big things, little things—

everything's a struggle." It is wrong and I feel sorry and scared immediately. I apologize and we hug but I'm full of sick regret. While collating the cruel cognitions, Joshua spins me around with hands clutching my shoulders, "Mom, stop thinking about the could'ves, would'ves, should'ves. You have me now; you can see me, touch me; even if I end up dead, you have me now."

Things feel back in sync. But I'm still reserved with my friend. Planning to keep up casual, yet surface connection until the healing is complete, but true reconciliation seems remote. I don't enjoy her anymore. Is that the benchmark of friendship? Do I feel better or worse after encounters?

Joshua's court date has been postponed until December. He may go immediately to jail. Boy, I've come a long way. Instead of crying a bucket, I separate the events of the past without making them an all-consuming focus of the present. Joshua looks and acts healthy. But explosive arguments come out of nowhere, their roots embedded in old fears and resentments—some conscious, some not. Joshua walks into the room. I'm doing paperwork and he gets a call. He hangs up and I ask quietly, "Was that a Marine recruiter?" He explodes, "NO WAY!" Am I looking at blatant using behavior or is it dry drunk rancor?

Minutes later he announces he will take a few days off to rest from his job because he's worked so hard and everybody does it. With lips peeled and fangs showing, I snarl, "You don't need to take a break! You need to pay back everyone you owe." It erupts into an ugly scene as he countersinks an insult and the flying gunk stains my mood. He goes on, "Why can't you like me the way I am?" Holding back but thinking, *I can't like you. I don't like or respect you. I love you, but cannot, will not, like you unconditionally.* He continues, "Oh I know, I've got to kiss your ass or you'll send me packing."

46

How true it is. He says he doesn't have freedom. True again. He gave it up when he crawled back. Our argument ends and he pivots and leaves. Dropping to a crouch, sobs squirt from my soul. The disease fractures the strongest bonds between parent and child.

*   *   *

Joshua comes home on time but I smell alcohol on his breath. He looks me in the eye and denies it. I push harder, "I will not kick you out if you tell me the truth." He bows his head and admits it. The fight this morning was a convenient excuse. My guilt returns—did I set him up? No. I'm not responsible for his recovery, nor is he for mine. This is a solitary journey. It is this routine we know so well: adjusting the ballast, buttering the bricks. I threaten, confront, retract and forgive.

Bob and I want him to finish the job at the fair—he never finishes anything. We rationalize our decision saying it was a small slip. He regrets it and wants to keep on track. Today he will probably work and stay sober. I do not feel the tide turning and I almost always sense the shift. We're doing the waiting game—just waiting, waiting for his next rehab. We haven't given up hope—not yet. But every time I achieve equanimity, something knocks me off-balance. Keeping the secret helps stabilize the load. I compartmentalize and keep my professional and private life separate. I go to work and feel protected in a cocoon, which offers momentary peace. I don't have to look at myself and more importantly, *reveal* me. My true self... the grieving, fearful, shame-filled Karla can be hidden for a few hours. I'm hesitant to disclose the secret for I feel it is a confession of failure. Most behavior is driven by the avoidance of pain, but healing is coming out of hiding.

When the shelling stops the eye of the storm presents a false sense of security and in some ways is more portentous than when the desolation flies. The *waiting* keeps one stuck.

47

Too weary, worried and wrecked to abandon ship we wait and drift. Up goes the periscope when I hear his key in the door. I listen closely to the footfalls. The pace and speed of his walk forewarn what mood will flood the room. He says he's going to meetings. Who knows? Two things I'm certain of: he doesn't want to be thrown out and he doesn't want to go to jail.

I still harbor animosity toward my "so-called" friend. True, I miss the good times but bad times outweigh them. I'm shielded from the judgment, slurs, name-calling and gossip. I'm buffered too from the bragging that stings my jealous heart and from the future pain when my child continues to screw up and her children rocket to greater heights. And if mine should turn out okay or even lap the pack, I will not boast but bow with gratitude.

A couple moved in across the street. Ordinarily, I would bring cookies and a smile to a new neighbor's front door, but that was back when. While mowing his lawn, the man introduces himself before I can make a quick escape. Within seconds he announces his son just got his master's in something from somewhere. What a turnoff. Was that the real reason he stopped, to brag, not to meet and greet? I'm tempted to say, "Oh, how nice. Our son is a high school dropout and a meth addict. But my husband and I have master's degrees, how 'bout you?"

When life was going well, envy was a manageable and uncommon emotion. However, once joy seemed permanently erased, jealousy tattooed my sad heart. We envy when we compare and hold up our existence to others. To envy we must first measure and then in the comparison, find we are lacking. I am the mother of an addict rather than a healthy son. But envy is a signal to face reality and it either motivates change or acceptance. The agony is in the imaginings of a future that will remain as painful as the present.

48

Envy motivated me to change what I could. But somewhere was an unrealistic expectation I would get what I deserved. I worked hard for it. Tried long and dedicated everything to it, and yet it was, as someone else described... "A life infected by disease, crossing generations and laughing at the futility."

I crawl out of bed late—another restless night obsessing. Announcement on TV: A nineteen-year-old is shot and killed during a party with over one hundred kids. God, help and comfort the family whose time was up. I'm full of longing for long ago and up ahead, if over the ridge means better not worse. But Joshua's appointment to schedule treatment is postponed. It's put off by another ten days... another ten days of waiting. Although he's restless, Joshua stays in his adult and doesn't explode like a toddler leaving a toy store empty-handed.

*   *   *

We have a pleasant stretch for three weeks— a family weekend at the beach creates improved memories. Because Joshua's pink cloud lures him from contracts, we clamp down and he's been compliant. But grief still surfaces. Walking hand-in-hand with Bob last evening we stroll by Joshua's former middle school. As the varsity football bus heads off to the game, trailing behind in eager anticipation are parents one after another, full of excitement, pride and hope. We had been there once. We clutch each other briefly as our faces fill with sorrow. Like a black hole, the disease changes the trajectory of your life. Black holes are unseen until things are pulled into their darkness. Although invisible, they bend light and give themselves away. Gravity gone mad becomes powerful. The heavier something is, the harder it is to escape its force.

Addiction is self-imposed exile. As you walk away from the world, you withdraw from people and avoid inviting them to your home. Fear of detection is paramount. Actual humiliations reinforce this and the pattern becomes entrenched. During a reprieve, you may feel sociable and plan a party or dinner, but when trouble erupts the regret is overwhelming. How can you back out and not draw attention to the family secret? Eventually the risk is too great, and at all costs you avoid having outsiders in your home—overnight, for an evening or an hour.

Now, all the literature will tell you this is classic, dysfunctional behavior. Just go ahead and have that party; if your child comes in, vomits on a guest or two, or if the sheriff rings the doorbell during dessert, don't apologize—simply say, "Oh well, our kid's an addict and these interruptions are common here." I guarantee that will have them packing out the door or perhaps open self-disclosures of their own...but don't count on it. You're not the only one who keeps secrets.

*   *   *

The disease creates shadow stains. While sleeping in Saturday morning, the doorbell rings, urgent and persistent. Foggy, I try to process and make sense of the disturbance. Again, again, the bell rings and rings. Now it hits—oh my God, it's the authorities to tell us Joshua's been hurt, shot or died of an overdose! I peek down stairs and make out a tall figure in a dark uniform, back- lit behind the glass. "Bob, Bob," I squeak, my voice crimped with fear. "There's someone at the door; you need to do this, you need to be with me." He doesn't stir, and again the persistent ring, ring, ring!

I slowly descend the stairs, open the door and brace when I see its Jason showing off his first solo run as a UPS driver. He looks so proud in his uniform; it diminishes the terror and pulls me back from hell. I grab him as much out of pride and joy as relief. Once again I thank God and stand dumbfounded as this disease colors everything. Later, I tell Bob how I resented going to the door alone. What if it had been dreadful news? I needed him. I needed his hand to hold.

50

Joshua left this morning for his second in-patient. He used all weekend, came home high, pupils blown and minimizing it was only a couple of beers and a Vicodan. This is a waste of time. He's determined to self-destruct. Bob's coping better or his denial thicker, not sure which, not sure of anything except likely outcomes. I watch a TV documentary about an execution but can't finish. A mother's son is killed for killing someone else. There are worse things than this. Please, don't let me know of them.

Joshua phoned from rehab sounding good. He's made a friend, likes his counselor, no appealing girls and spoke of growth and recovery. If only we could hold on to this moment and have it carry us forward and settle like a fuzzy blanket fresh from the dryer.

Friends from Al-Anon dropped by Saturday night and we had a pleasant dinner. It's nice to connect with people who relate. Sunday's Al-Anon elicited a confession. I admitted out loud to a room full of strangers my chief defects: envy, perfectionism and shame. It wasn't difficult and I saw several heads nod with understanding. Getting honest is getting free.

*   *   *

We drive to the treatment center to visit Joshua. When we pull up he is looking out a window with his million-watt smile. As we go into our first group lecture, he hugs and kisses us. But at break time we take a walk around the grounds and he shares his goals, which includes another HIV test. This frightens me, initiating immediate tears. Just why is this important to know right now? Yes, if he is HIV positive we will support him through the end of his life. But what if he's negative? I will have to ride out this next stretch. The fear never lets up.

It's not my intention to tell Joshua about our new curfew when he comes home, however the timing seems right and as he prepares us, we prepare him. His reaction is

51

predictable—anger, sulking and trudging away. For just an instant we take the bait but rational thought saves us.

In the family group, without Joshua there, we discuss what transpired—only minutes earlier enjoying a warm reunion and now enduring our son's silence. About an hour later he comes around, which demonstrates remarkable growth or enormous fear—perhaps both. We leave with good feelings and guarded optimism but fully enjoy, love and live through the day.

* * *

Disappointment bears witness to this disease. It's Apple Cup at Washington State University, an annual football competition between Washington State University and the University of Washington. I once dreamed Joshua would play football for one of the teams; instead, he sits in drug rehab. Instead of frat parties and cramming for finals, he must be in bed at 10:00 o'clock to stay out of jail.

Joshua gets out of rehab tomorrow. I look at the welcome- home banner hung across the fireplace mantle. If Joshua was returning after a different illness, the banner would be proudly displayed front porch and center. But *this* banner will be placed away from prying and judgmental eyes.

Progress is marked by the tiniest increments, yet improvements real and measurable. I have slept well most nights and had only one, small relapse. Joshua's homecoming heralds nothing but live-in-the-moment happiness. He is full of enthusiasm and riding the crest of success. I beam, yet hold back —this is an all-too-typical venue not to be mistaken for reality, which will soon set in.

His old friends know within hours, if not minutes of his arrival and one has already called. This will be his nemesis. He deludes himself thinking he can choose to see certain friends who will honor his recovery. I figure we have two to three weeks. We're waiting for him to step out of the glow and into the world of temptations. Joshua asks me to read his treatment homework. I comply but now regret it. Does he seek absolution or want to punish me? Is it an attempt to prepare us for the inevitable, to further break denial or to relate from a place of perfect honesty?

My happiness is short-lived replaced with crushing dread. A similar terror when I walked the long corridor that led to my mother's deathbed the night she left this world. This monster is only sleeping. I feel its breath bearing down. We can evade it only temporarily; it will awaken. I feel imminent collapse, the exact time and day unknown but outcome sure and certain. Will he die quickly, slowly, take others with him, cry out, whimper, linger and suffer or exist one second and be gone the next? Do we have years, months, weeks or days?

Joshua home not forty-eight hours and already hooking up with a friend, but one who will respect his recovery. Yeah, we've heard that before. He plans to see a movie and wants money but we refuse. He'll get it from his buddy. I ask if his friend has a job. Joshua defends him and I mumble under my breath. Joshua's anger comes up, "Just say what's on your mind!"

Carefully, I choose the words, "Yes, I'm a little leery of your friend because he's an addict. No, I don't think you want to use tonight but if you hang with him eventually resistance will loosen."

"Mom! I'm not going to use."

"I didn't say you were, I just think it's risky." Going on I add, "Now if I'm not getting better, how come the psycho bitch isn't demanding you stay home? I'm simply making an observation," I say, as he walks out the door. Just this morning he said, "Mom, I want you to call me on my bullshit." Well, *this* is bullshit—his first couple of days out of rehab and he's not at a meeting, he's with an addict. *That's* bullshit.

I fall to the floor and sob. From the edge of my mind I see doom waiting in the shadows. The tears come from knowing what might be, the realization of what has been and what hell lies ahead. The contrast is stark and terrifying. Every time he relapses it's worse than the last.

Jason asked about my friend today. I was vague; don't really want to discuss it and leave him too with bad feelings. I prefer to let him remember her in a positive way. I think that's important. I also don't want to re-open old wounds. I miss her and wonder if she misses me. I wish she could have loved me like a sister. Perhaps it was unrealistic. Maybe friends can never love like family. But I too, did not love well. Love does not boast but it also does not envy. We excuse to the degree we love. Want a friend? Marry one.

* * *

Today Joshua got good results from the HIV test. Thank God we rolled past this one, but can I imagine the rest of my life this way? Joshua said he wasn't worried but he's nineteen. What do they worry about? How can I choose serenity in the midst of this maelstrom? How do I fold recovery into my life? I look at my reflection and see a tired woman beaten by fear, a mere shadow of my former self, confident and beaming. How do I bring life back to its former luster? No longer able to focus clearly, sad eyes see everything in subdued light.

Joshua phoned the next night and said he would be late —not even two weeks home and rules already broken. I don't pay attention to excuses because it's impossible to know what's true. Knew this morning would probably be trouble. I set an earlier curfew and he called me a warden. Living with his resentments and mine is like walking on broken glass. Yes, I wish he were well and could move out, and yes, I set boundaries and start battles. He hates me for hating the disease that makes me hateful.

Joshua goes to court and is read the riot- act. If he offends one more time he will go directly to jail for two years. He also has another two-year probation, $550 fine and ten-day work crew. He never gets out of the hole.

I'm glad I've pulled away from my friend. I don't have to rehash the details. Marooned on a barren atoll, normal life ended when gored by the dagger. Finding myself awake, yet in a nightmare, I pass a mirror and look at a stranger's face. It leaves me unable to recognize myself or remember my purpose.

Joshua finds a job, but the biggest hurdle, keeping it. He went to a meeting last night and shared about another person in his after-care group, a twenty-six-year-old woman who just lost her job and was full of fear facing her parents (yes, she still lives at home) and her possible relapse. Joshua was really talking about his own fears and I leaned in and listened intently. I pointed out he is not responsible for our happiness, nor are we for his. If he loses this job he has choices and so do we and wouldn't it be important to look at unconscious motives, fear of failure, fear of success and a way to set one's self up in order to use?

I'm not excited or worried. It was a pleasant day and I will enjoy this one problem-free day—not bring the grief of the past or the dread of tomorrow in to pollute it. If he relapses this time and is arrested for anything, he will go to jail for two years...a fact, not a feeling...but a future possibility, not eventuality and therefore not a fact *today*.

* * *

I find a message on the machine from my friend. Is it because I accidentally called her and she has Caller ID? Or was I hoping to get stuff off my chest? I return the call and leave a message asking her to call again. An apology would mean so much. She calls back but the conversation ruptures. I mention how I've been hurting and she responds, "Well, this may sound mean, but I'm glad you've been hurting because

I've been hurting, too." It's a cruel cut. But she also lets me know how much it stung when I hadn't gone to her party, criticized her daughter-in-law and how she was getting fed up with me.

I'm fed up too, and accuse her of bragging, verbal abuse and disloyal gossip. She denies she brags and we hang up forever.

A MISSED OPPORTUNITY

Dear Former Friend,   *December 17, 1998*

I feel compelled to write what has been too difficult to discuss in detail. I am still recovering from what I perceive as a major wound. You might be happy to know, as you told me on the phone, I am still hurting, but perhaps you have struggled in your own way.

For several months I have felt hurt, unloved, condescended to, disrespected, judged, labeled, vilified and patronized. This has altered my impression of our friendship.

Not wanting mute contempt to continue to breed petty vengeance, I have pulled away. At one time I felt our friendship was as close as sisters and I relied on that loyalty, but it was an illusion. I've lost trust and have learned, because you reminded me, of my **real** *place.*

I feel betrayed that you and your daughter-in-law gossiped behind our backs. Perhaps you were conflicted about approaching us. But did it ever occur to you we just might not have known about Joshua and withholding that information was unconscionable? And to add insult to injury, you listened while I confessed this secret and all the time you knew it!

As I searched where this friendship unraveled, that conversation a couple of years ago about staying at your condo was the turning point. To refresh your memory, it was you who offered the condo to us and then suddenly retracted the invitation. Was that because you had just learned about Joshua? It was also during that conversation when you first called me a dufus and said I wasn't really family. As you recall, I tried to defend myself, but I was stunned and scared of what was happening.

I now take full responsibility for not confronting you immediately—such as, "Hey, that really hurt and I'm confused; I thought we were family. You've said we were; you're in our wills to raise the kids if we die! What's this really about? And, "Please don't call me a dufus; it's mean and hurtful."

Upon reflection, I wonder if your reluctance to have us use the condo was not only because your son and daughter-in-law wanted it that weekend (although you offered it to us first) but also because they heard from their babysitter who attended Joshua's school that he is a drug addict. And did you call me a dufus because you disrespected my denial or ignorance of the problem?

While tracing the roots of this estrangement, I have taken a fearless moral inventory. I was overly dependent and relied on you for emotional support. I envied you and others with healthy families because I didn't grow up in one and don't enjoy one now. I have also resented your bragging, born of my recent insecurities. As my life crumbled it became more difficult for me to celebrate your success. I stuffed my feelings like a coward. Having kept those feelings inside, they showed up in petty put-downs of your daughter-in-law, for which I am truly sorry.

I have been overly sensitive and have had unrealistic expectations, but I never criticized your daughter-in-law behind your back, although many of your friends have.

I have resented your contempt and faultfinding in me when it is ignored and dismissed in others. I am quick to anger and slow to forgive. I am flawed and defective, but isn't everyone? I wish you well and will try to fondly remember the good times.   *Sincerely, Karla*

I thought it was safe to turn to a friend when I was hurting. We had been acquainted for eighteen years, but I was just getting to know her. Once as close as sisters, I found myself fleeing the relationship. I told myself I was in pursuit of authenticity, which in part was true. But moreover, I was doing what I did best: When the going gets tough, I build walls, burn bridges and push people away.

When my friend called me a name, it was a bowel adhesion, kinking and gripping my gut. When she tooted her horn, it chaffed a raw and runny wound. But honest analysis forces a fuller explanation. It wasn't so much her bragging, she had always done that, it was the deep and dark trench I was in. What had once been mildly irritating became excruciating as my opportunities for happiness seemed closed forever. My needs and expectations weren't revealed until the end, which ultimately detonated the friendship. Boasting, as someone described, fans the fires of envy and the chemistry turns combustible. Criticism of my friend and her daughter-in-law was my anger and pain surfacing in ugliness. Mistakenly, I believed friendship meant I could bare my soul with impunity. But oh no, friendships *are* conditional. They involve important and unspoken rules. True friendship requires we forgive and be forgiven. Somewhere in time I learned it was hard to forgive and dangerous to show anger. To express anger was to risk abandonment.

Being called a "dufus" and "not family" left me feeling disrespected and fearful. But it was my fault leaving the vituperation unresolved. Lots of choices we make and behaviors we enact are beyond our awareness. I was still operating out of fear, like when I was frightened by my violent father. I was well aware of her abuse but couldn't defend myself. Instead I pushed her away.

I have only experienced conditional love with friends. When I did what was expected I was lovable. However, if I didn't do what was expected, I was unlovable. It's comforting to know I am worthy and worthwhile, whether or not I meet someone's expectation. But this applies to both parties. Friendships are clogged with gridlocks as friends steer clear of all but the safest emotions. It was wishful thinking to expect her to run interference. I learned to build walls, not bridges and often sabotaged myself. But now I no longer stuff feelings. What was routine with family was new and terrifying with friends. Now, I check what I'm thinking. Is it distorted? Is it propelled by character defects? Are my intentions to contribute or contaminate the relationship? Do I want to stop a behavior or end a friendship?

I still struggle when I sense someone's anger. My fears come up and I wonder if they will abandon me. I must guard my worth so it does not plummet by their actions. If they too have demons, I must ask myself if I want to remain with people who are also fearful of confrontation and passive/aggressive. Can I remember others value me and continue to do so in spite of my mistakes? Can I remember I can't please all of the people all of the time? I am the sum total, not specific dependent. I am a person of infinite capacity and so are you. Good or bad, can I remember to be gentle, as I would want the same? If I expect to be loved, I must be lovable.

Upon reflection, I never would have admitted my flaws had my hand not been forced. Pain pried opened my mind.

*   *   *

Bouncing back, I remind Joshua to pick up his cigarette butts in the flowerbed. Bob and I don't smoke making the eyesore irritating. Joshua yells and stomps through the room, "All you do is nag, nag, nag!" What agenda is this? Is it a smoking gun or a mushroom cloud? Is the demon resurrected and living in our midst? The disease is punishing, creating fissures that are chronic.

Today is New Year's Eve and my fiftieth birthday. We planned an out of town celebration, but I can barely get out of bed—not a mid-life crisis, but a mid-addiction one. We found a note when we woke up. Joshua's taken off and flicks us like a toothpick.

Addictions don't take vacations. Like embolisms, they block life. One minute you're alive looking forward to the trip; the next nothing but the death rattle. Dead mother walking. Dead at fifty.

THREE

Darkness & Despair

1999

Today I left my clothes in a heap on the floor. I didn't make the bed or put the dishes in the sink. That's not me, but I'm sit-and-do-nothing sad. Yesterday was my cruelest birthday. New Year's Eve is a time of revelry and self-absorption. People forget, pre-empt, postpone or delay something meaningful to me. And if they are addicts, the oversights are multiplied. They don't just forget to call but minimize their rude neglect.

Chemicals disregard and override and compel before ingested and dominate and linger long after. Apologies declare no malicious intent, but tell that to the mother sawed in half by the self-centered drunk.

It's occasions like this that slash open the sorrow. I could always tell myself he loved me and that helped make up for the rest, but even that has proved an exaggeration. Pain is only conquered when set firmly on the back of truth. With each blow I lose more of myself. Each oversight blots and blurs the cornerstone, which kept me anchored. I must prepare a canvas to accept what is and can't and won't ever be. I must examine how I set myself up and tip myself over; splatter when no one is looking and how I must be my own mop and bucket.

Chemicals have, do and will take precedence over everything and everyone. That certainly includes you and me even on our birthdays. Rather than pay tribute to our beginnings, it's more of a thorn in their compulsive sides; a reminder they are slaves to the crave and we're held in contempt for being born different.

Where shall I go? What should I do? I must single-handedly answer those questions. I can rant and suck my thumb or thumb my nose. I can go on or call it quits. I can read or write or shop until I feel loved enough. I can feel sorry for myself forever or chalk it up to another drop in the bucket. Makes no difference—the scourge will endure. It's too big, too dark and too selfish.

* * *

My fear is and always has been Joshua's death—permanent, indelible, irreversible death. When he called with his belated birthday greeting, I tried to get him to come home with tears, intimidation and every relapsing trick in my worn-out book—but of course I failed. Only talking to an Al-Anon friend and getting to a meeting have kept me from slipping further into the abyss. It was a *very* close call. What have I learned? The second I recognize fear and sadness returning get to a meeting and fight it. Drop everything and *drag* myself out the door. It saved my life. Someone asked, "Is cracking up really breaking through?"

* * *

Joshua finally comes home but the tension is thick and electric. Everything he does, says, even the way he moves irritates me. I'm sticky with anger and can hardly be civil. Nothing gets between a mother and child like addiction.

All day I've been irritable, faultfinding, bitter and obsessed with all that is wrong in our lives. When did life get so hard? When did I give up? I isolate more and more, don't even hug or cuddle with Bob, spend less time with the cat, rarely answer the phone and run and hide when the doorbell rings. The effort to conduct a small conversation is almost too much. Yet, I'm not thinking of death—just how to recapture my elusive self, how to jump-start my soul.

Joshua is fired again from the latest job. This time he held it less than a week. Are we prepared to go on like this forever? Fear snaps at our heels like a rat terrier. It deepens my depression and freezes me in place.

Is chemical addiction a way to control others and mask fear? Do people drug to avoid responsibility or is it purely psychological? Many authorities disagree, saying it's first a physical disease that erodes mind, body and spirit, not a primary psychological condition; sick people don't become addicts but become sick after they drink and drug.

All I know is I love my son and my heart aches for whatever is holding him back. He was created to soar. I don't want to lose him so I guess I've made my choice to go on this way a bit longer, even though with every excuse, I lose more of myself. I'm the classic co-dependent, placing his needs before my own.

Walking the plank, I woke several times last night. Earlier, Joshua came home with pupils like inkblots, denying meth and forgetting his court-ordered counseling. I started to talk, but what's the point? Like a cat with a mouse, the torture is slow and the results hideous.

Do you feel like you're thrown to the lions? Someone described the following:

The Roman Coliseum seated over a fifty thousand people who were provided marble tickets and watched elaborate acts of violence and pageantry. The wooden floor was covered in sand to soak the blood, while maidens sprinkled perfume to control the stench. Below was an immense network of dark tunnels that housed criminals, slaves, gladiators and starving wild animals. Everything from mock floods to battle scenes, complete with intricate sets, was erected for entertainment.

Addiction, like Titus, stages greater and more ghastly spectacles trans-forming life into ever more grisly scenes, labyrinths dark and foreboding, where human cargo awaits platform hoists to lift them to their slaughter. Victims daubed with blood guarantee the mauling while baying crowds cheer with glee and belch their lunch.

*   *   *

The next weekend Joshua's dropped off and stumbles through the front door drunk, obnoxious, cursing and lamenting. He sleeps it off, remembers little and apologizes for nothing. Recovery accepts life without regret. Painful tutelage: Addicts are neither good nor bad, they just are.

Joshua senses we're ready to evict him; therefore a period of calm revives us. Although he's still not working, he talks of plans and responsibilities, giving us a peek at a better future. We soak his charm with blurry hope, but before we know it, we're getting sick, sick, sick, quick, quick, quick.

Meanwhile, back in hell, Joshua doesn't come home again. He starts a new job tomorrow. The next day he begs for forgiveness and promises he'll try harder. But like a plodding mule stopped abruptly, I remember people swallow spiders while they sleep.

This decent into madness has taken me from adoring my son to barely being able to look at him. Subject to the push and pull of the monster, the assassin gains momentum. I beat it off, but it's like sweeping the ocean back with a broom.

I once was an out-going person and had a wide circle of friends. Now I brood and resent everything and everyone. I sit in this squalor and curse God and beg his forgiveness in a single breath.

I used to be a happy, warm wife. Now I drone about our son or become bitchy with the slightest provocation. Like today when Bob, who's a computer consultant, is helping me with new software. Exasperated with my picky whining, he evacuates the office refusing to hand-hold any longer when I bark, "Just how am I supposed to cut and paste this shit if my teacher leaves class to suck his thumb?"

Shrugging the projection, he throws his voice from the other room, "Figure it out yourself!" Incensed, I think…see if I reboot your hard drive tonight, as I push every button on the PC willing it to die, expecting the robotic voice to say, "Initiating pissed off sequence." For a second I consider pouring the rest of my soda on the keyboard but veto that as my pragmatic self wins. *Everything* irritates me. But amazingly, Bob stands by during the worst erosion.

Last night Joshua didn't check in or even have a friend call. I hope he was arrested so he can't blame us when we put him out. The anxiety is similar to major surgery. Something is cut from life and like a disease devours from the inside out, tear ducts are gone so you cry from the heart.

At 12:30 A.M. the next morning, a girl calls on his behalf letting us know he's okay, as opposed to dead, I imagine. At least the guilt is gone about evicting him. He chose his critical deployment. Unremitting, time shakes us by the shoulders. We've waited long enough; held on long enough; hung in long enough; put up long enough. It's time.

Is this what it's like for mothers waiting for sons to return from war? Hoping they come home full of promise, not perish on a distant beach or unknown shore? Day in, day out, waiting and praying for good news—not flesh ripped open by metal explosions or fragments blown to smithereens?

Did Roman mothers cry unexpectedly and double in grief? Did they fall to their knees begging for the wave to pass? Did they sniff their son's clothing and hold it close and will his safe return? Did they wake at night and repeat his name? Did they think about his hunger or imagine his thirst? Did they understand the battles and fears he faced? Did their lamentations compose a collective chronicle for all mothers for all times? Can anyone but another mother know what it is like?

Lugging his belongings, Joshua is tearful and turns for a moment into a scared little boy as he stands on our front porch. How difficult to see him face his battle, but we have no other choice for him, for us.

He said none of his friends could put him up and he had a court date in the morning. What could he do—no alarm clock—where would he sleep? Although it tugged at our hearts, we were loving, kind but assertive. We don't care one-way or the other if he makes it to court. It's no longer our problem. He asked if he proved he had worked for a month would we let him come back. A month isn't nearly enough. Six months would be unheard of and only prove he is a functioning addict.

We've learned every time we help him we delay devastation and the gift of despair, which raises his bottom and possible surrender and recovery. By gently removing the support system, we release loving duress. We don't know what the future holds. We pray God will restore and heal him, but now we're focused on ourselves.

I went to a meeting tonight. Al-Anon is a nice satchel to carry the pain. I cried, disclosed and reached for help and help was there. I'm at the right place. Although drained, I feel renewed and liberated. As Bob and I rebuild our lives, we pray for Joshua, for us, for everyone affected by this disease and for *you*, dear parent in pain.

Joshua came by a few days later and wailed about his predicament. He was flushed with fear although he got another "stay from going to jail" (yes, he got to court on time) but we didn't ask how. We talked for a while and then he left, knowing his room and board would not be reinstated. But, I can't stop shaking. My son is out there tonight in thirty-two degrees. Somehow, he has to face this alone, and in order to help, we mustn't help at all. The perverse irony opens a vein and leaves us dripping without tourniquets.

More days pass and Joshua blows in—urgent, distant and matter-of-fact. He's impossible to reach. I slip, "You know Joshua, the day may come when we won't have time or interest in you. How do you suppose that will make you feel?" He denies he's using, but I can tell now when he lies and he turns away in shame.

Verbal camouflage once impaled me, but now I see through his lies. But as I evolved and set new boundaries, at first they were cloaked in contempt. It took time to teach my heart the difference between detachment and hostile withdrawal. I remind myself with this letter:

Dear Karla,

You blew it. Try to remember Joshua is young, very young, and more importantly, really sick. Be grateful he wants to come by and as he often reminds you; be glad you have him alive.

Stop future tripping. Stop catastrophizing. And stop thinking the worst. Yes, it may be years, decades, before you hear or see any real improvement but work your program.

If what he says stirs too many emotions, gently tell him you're sorry, but you can't be his sponsor and try to talk about something pleasant. Touch him. Hold him. Tell him more than once how much you love him and how much you enjoy seeing him. You do enjoy seeing him— even though you dread addiction.

Stop punishing him for lack of progress—you aren't doing so hot relapsing left and right. Make it a nice experience and he probably will hug and kiss you good-bye. Try to fake it until you make it with inspiration, support and abundant regard.

Remember you are the adult and start modeling it.

Joshua deserves your love. He's a good boy with a bad disease and doesn't deserve to be disparaged. When you see him next time, hug him, love him and show compassion.

Karla

I wonder how long it will take to awaken in the morning and not anxiously descend the stairs. Not tentatively turn the corner and look for the answering machine flashing, not fear the call that comes in the night or waits each day. I wonder if I will ever go a full twenty-four hours without the fear piercing through and through. When can I pass his picture hanging on the wall and not stop and sigh, stop to regret?

Joshua calls to say "Hi." I never fully believe anything he says, so question privately his real intent. He chats and promises to stop by after counseling, but I won't hold my breath. If he shows up, fine; if he gets a job, fine; if he gets well, great; if he doesn't, he doesn't.

Detachment isn't desertion. Like what someone shared, "I've stopped waiting for the day when his eyes will open and I can look into his soul and see everything come into soft focus." I've learned my behavior has no effect on the disease. No matter what I do or don't do, say or don't say I am powerless against this uninvited war. The acid test of my recovery is measured by his relapsing behaviors. I don't go down as deep or stay as long.

Last evening we had another couple over to our house. It was nice and yet I frequently watched the clock and wanted to be elsewhere. Although I long for social contact, I rarely enjoy it. It puzzles and disquiets me at the same time. I'm reminded of Picasso when he said, "...entertaining visitors makes me tired."

Joshua called just after the company left and first I was alarmed but then pleasantly surprised. He sweetly thanked us over and over again and expressed gratitude for standing by him when so many families of addicts wash their hands.

I told him regardless of what he did, it would never change our love, and whether he recovered or if the disease claimed his life, we would be there for him to the end.

68

Always so unsure of what to say and how to say it, hoping the words help—not harm.

But Joshua continues to spin spokes of insanity, migrating from the irrational to the ridiculous. His latest plan and rabid height of hilarity is to go to airline training and be guaranteed employment. Five months of school and $4500 in tuition, room and board. Yeah, right. He's homeless, moving from friend to friend without a pot or window. The disease trumps convictions.

Another visit and Joshua appears introspective, less hyper and a little wistful. He still doesn't have direction but seems less flip and cavalier. Hints he wants to stay the night because he has an early probation appointment. He's pathetic and hands me an aching note but I'm not moved to tears. However, life's a dicey pulsar, threatening and warning: DANGER AHEAD - STEEP GRADE.

* * *

Having Joshua come by is grueling. I don't want him in the house. I've been upset all day. We obsess, argue and re-hash themes or sit with nothing to say until he gets up and walks out and leaves.

Grief throws me to the floor and I collapse into convulsive, baboon-like, barking sobs. I cover my mouth to muffle the yelps. All the sorrow explodes in a throaty scream. Bent and retching, I steady myself as the anguish rocks me.

Was this the breakthrough? Am I now fully prepared to accept addiction? Did this start or finish the grief? Hunched over and reeling, I sort the possibilities. I'm reminded once again; somewhere deep beneath the surface, a mantle of misery must and will erupt. I apologize to the cat crouched in the corner, eyes scared and confused. A pat on the head and then it's back to the front.

Next week Joshua may stop by. I hope I don't fill with anger, but genuine delight in seeing him, being with him for a few minutes. He may not show up and I prepare for that

69

too, knowing what it means and keeping faith.

Life otherwise is improving. Spring-cleaning is therapeutic and relaxing. It's nice to get life back *and* in order. As I write, it is not my intention to play victim but to process pain. The tears lubricate and limber as I retrain my rigid self. Chemical addiction is reason enough to legitimize sorrow. I'm not ashamed. I no longer apologize for my acting out. The antidote for grief is grieving. When your heart's broken, but still beating, hold on, hang in and hike out.

While rethinking the route, I obsess less, sleep great and spend a relaxing weekend with Bob in a harbor village. But when something good happens, experience tells me it won't last.

* * *

Joshua's in a city three hours from home. His employer has put him and his two friends up in a nice motel and will give them a pay advance while they train in new jobs. Joshua's excited but worried if he can hang in and not lose interest; if he can stay clean and sober.

I pray night and day. He has to juggle counseling, probation and court appearances. He doesn't want his boss to know the particulars. The guys need an apartment, but they're okay tonight. I've learned full well things can change in a minute. For now Bob and I tell no one, which isn't difficult because so few ask.

Joshua comes home for Bob's fiftieth birthday in conjunction with a court appointment. He looks healthy but the job worries me—dangerous haz-mat. Six people died last year, now it all fits. There had to be a catch. There always is. I prayed hard for this to work out and now I pray it won't kill him. If it doesn't last, I don't care. As we said our good-byes I hugged him a special long embrace. He expressed fear he might mess up at any time and drove to his future.

It's nice to unwind for a couple days. Joshua phoned last night and said he'd be by with friends to get his

70

household goods and drive to his new apartment. We jumped through our butts to prepare, only to have him call later saying they weren't coming. He called back early the next morning and said while driving to work, his right rear tire fell off his car. Thank God, he was going slowly, near a phone and it didn't happen the night before on the freeway going 70 mph in the dark. Within two days we replaced his muffler $73.00, towed him $70.00 and fixed a bearing and something else for $133.00. I was called out of class three times and another time while unloading groceries on a conveyer belt.

I'm reminded of that old joke: When a norm's (non alcoholic/addict) car breaks down, they call a tow truck, when an addict's car conks out, they call their dealer. Is it progress when they call their parents? We enable because he is working and trying hard although good behavior doesn't guarantee clemency.

But such a lovely reprieve the next day, the kind of day that momentarily transports us in time and place. A scrumptious lunch in a lodge by cascading falls tumbling into a gorge...a fresh flower on a tiny table, wine by a crackling fire and endearing words from the man I love. A day of brief rains and more frequent sun-breaks...a reversal of fortune, a renewal of spirit. Perhaps life is worth living. We emerge from hibernation and see a life incinerated, but like a morning mist hovers a new garden, green and curious, we're hungry to heal.

*   *   *

Joshua's latest call reports he's still employed, but burned out. He complains he no longer has a life (translation, he can no longer screw off). The boys were rejected from the first apartment and will have to settle for a less fancy one. Their background check caught up with them and reality has set in. What we do today we have to live with tomorrow. Now that his car is operational, we rarely hear from him. He still hasn't come to get all his possessions. Maybe we'll see him this weekend. It would be nice because Sunday is Easter. When he does call, he's tired and affectionate but resigned and disappointed with his choices: work, go to prison or be a bum.

A new message on the machine says Joshua will be home Friday night to give us a "presentation of his feelings." It's been over three weeks, just long enough on the new job to quit and move on. This doesn't come as a surprise. We like our independence and won't go quietly back into the dark.

Poor Joshua lost in delirium. He's in crisis again. He quit the job and asks to stay with us but we refuse and recommend a shelter. I see the neighbors' boy leave for college. That could have been, should have been Joshua. Instead, our son slept in his car. Each day, a wasted day, and I must detach with love and learn to accept the things I cannot change. Learning this is counter to second nature. Mothers are hard- wired to alleviate suffering.

* * *

Our first social gathering of non Al-Anons will be here Sunday after Bob's softball game. I know I'll be nervous. A part of me worries the disease will intrude on the afternoon. But now we organize, plan and look forward to engagements. We don't have to learn, as much as remember how to relate.

But it's a short hop to the next argument with you know who. Joshua says he can't get a ride to pick up his car. I reply, "So?" Then continue with unleashed fury, "Don't you dare tell me you can't get a ride. You can hustle anyone for anything." CLICK. He hangs up and I hear the high school bus squeak to a stop in front of our house. Joshua missed that bus and life left him behind.

But these troubles can't compare to tragedy at a Colorado school: Two disturbed kids kill more than a dozen—born of revenge. My heart cries for all, but most for the parents of the shooters. They will be blamed and yet their pain is probably the greatest. Not only did they lose their sons (both took their own lives) but they had children who committed unspeakable crimes and caused terrible sorrow.

While preparing breakfast, I listened to "Good Morning America." Charlie Gibson and Diane Sawyer have a segment where they comment on news worthy topics. Referring to Littleton, Colorado, Charlie Gibson said although the shooters' seemed to come from loving, good homes, "Was there something the parents missed; signs they didn't pick up on?" (Sure, you miss things—what parent doesn't?) Of course this holds parents responsible for their children's choices, blaming the very people whose hearts are broken.

Mr. and Mrs. Klebold and Mr. and Mrs. Harris, I want you to know there are people who don't blame or judge you. You probably did the best you could. Your sons made conscious, willful decisions to perpetrate those heinous crimes, and only they know why. Don't crucify yourselves. These boys were not only raised by you, but also raised by this society, in this world and in this lifetime. They are separate and unique, with experiences, dispositions and strengths and weaknesses entirely theirs and theirs alone.

Those who condemn haven't walked in difficult shoes—shoes that feel solid and comfortable, then suddenly vaporize beneath their feet.

* * *

It's always with a mixture of relief and apprehension when I begin a conversation with Joshua. So glad to know he's alive, but waiting for the bad news, and there's almost *always* bad news. Having devoured the first 124 pages of the A.A. Big Book, I listened with empathy when he divulged the latest problem: he was stopped for a burned-out headlight. I replied softly, "Gee, I'm sorry," and meant it. How he pays or if he pays is his problem. And if he lands in jail, that may be the very thing that moves him closer to surrender. He also mentioned he was seeking in-patient treatment again. He's only buying time, not really ready to stop, but the best I can do is step out of the way. I finished the conversation by inviting him to dinner. We'll see if he shows up. We'll wait and see about everything. He never showed up.

I listen to a business management lecture. We're all assigned a set of monkeys and it's our responsibility to care for and feed them. Life works when we take care of our own monkeys; where we get into trouble is when other people's monkeys become our responsibility. We need to focus on getting our own monkeys off our backs. Bob and I have entertained the idea to take in and care for capuchin monkeys trained to assist quadriplegics. Little furry creatures, wearing diapers, toothless and harmless, funny and appealing. It makes perfect sense. No middle of the night emergencies; no arrests on our doorstep.

*   *   *

After several days of not talking to Joshua, I try to reach him. I'm surprised when he calls back, because he isn't aware of my previous attempts. He's on a binge quarantined in a cheap motel with addicts and needs to ask a favor. Why else would he call? Will I give him a wake-up ring in the morning, as he doesn't trust the flaky staff. I agree.

His appointment today is for rehab assessment. He also has court coming up for violation of probation, fines due in ten days or he will go to jail. He's over-whelmed and scared, but still not ready to get to A.A. He's using crank again. Maybe he needs to return to jail. He's foolishly squandered his chances—now he will face losing his license, too. The hole gets deeper and deeper, but where is the bottom?

Recovery is a path, not a destination. Joshua says he needs a ride to detox and will go to treatment in western Washington for sixty-seven days. Detox is a clinic to clean up for three or four days before rehab. Joshua reports he had a big cry when he said goodbye to friends. I respond, "I'm sorry—it must be so hard." He replies, "You have no idea."

Driving home I listen to a radio interview with a recovering addict. His advice: "Never give up and always show them love, kindness and honor." God must have wanted me to hear that; live that.

I take Joshua to detox this morning. He's tired and thin; his clothes, torn and dirty. Only his youth keeps him physically intact. The disease steals everything else. He and I are tearful, but for different reasons. My sadness linked to replays—his to giving up friends and chemicals.

That same night he calls. He wants to come home but toughs it out with the threat of long-term in-patient if he refuses detox compliance. And if he continues to use, he will go back to jail. Jail is like detox but even worse, bad food, awful beds and no privacy whatsoever.

The next night he sounds better, but the conversation struggles. There's so little to talk about that doesn't set us off.

He asks, "What other disease requires giving up your friends?"

I snap, "You're not the only one who suffers. We wait to identify your body or for you to make your cameo appearance or cursory call. Most of the time we feel neglected and terrified."

Although he's safe in detox, I dread the pink clouds morphing into hailstorms. Carefully I pack his belongings for the two-month stay. If I fold it just right, tuck in a favorite toiletry and another radio with earphones, it will make it easier, right? Let nothing be missed...cover all bases to insure the best possible outcome? HA! Just more fear-driven garbage. None of it matters. Just going through the motions and preparing for round three— his third attempt —just waiting and praying for the answer that never comes. No mix of medicine and muscle can deliver the goods. Just pulling on boots and going through the slop again.

*   *   *

The road back is bumpy, but the next week I go out with women from work to dinner and a lecture. I'm my old self and can hardly believe it—laughing, witty, warm and engaging. I come home and fall sound asleep. The following week I write this letter to Joshua in rehab:

> *Hi Honey,*   *May 10, 1999*
> *So how's it going? We went to the Auburn mall yesterday, then saw the movie, Wm. Shakespeare's "A Midsummer's Night Dream." It was wonderful. Once you get the hang of the old English, you would be amazed at his genius. The background music is Giuseppe Verdi's opera, "La Traviata," a tale of love, passion and heartbreak. Oh Joshua, I will play it for you when you come home. Your heart will soar.*
> *I'm enjoying getting caught up today. Will run errands, maybe weed and if I'm still frisky, stop off in the library. Last night I was thinking happy memories...the times I'd come home from school and you'd have the cutest, most colorful love notes on my pillow...and the time we were waiting for a wurst in Germany and you were three years old and getting impatient. I said, "We have to wait honey," and you replied, "Well, then, let's just hug and kiss." You really melt my heart. And then the time you ran that race with the running club—five miles up and downhill with your shoe unlaced and still came in first in your division! And now when I hear you compliment us and show and express your gratitude—so many wonderful memories.*
> *I pray you make it this time. When you're in*

76

recovery, it's like you've been out to sea for many long months and then pull into port. How we love to "have you back" because when you're gone, you're so very far away. You are an incredible person—always have been. You absolutely light up a room and magnetize a home with your enormous vitality. Your kindness, sweetness and affection are your most wonderful qualities. When you are "out to sea" we miss that most.

Remember honey how much we care. If we could, we'd change places with you. Never, ever give up.

All our love,   *Mom & Dad*

I'm coming home from a great weekend at an Al-Anon seminar. Bonding with friends, meeting new women and a marvelous setting made it fun and fulfilling. In addition, we saw Joshua yesterday and he is such a pleasure when he's not toxic.

But I still think about my estranged friend. Second-guess myself too. Did I do the right thing, the wrong thing, too much, too little, set limits too late? I hold back now. Will I ever trust again? Allow myself to be vulnerable? Transparent? But these are mute points, like Churchill's, "Terrible chilling words...too late."

The next weekend is a wonderful intermission from the wear-you-down, get-you-down, keep-you-down drudgery of plowing through the mud and muck of this disease. Joshua is his new, improved, sober self.

I call my cousin this morning to wish his son a happy birthday. My cousin asks about Joshua, but before I can say much he launches into a glib soliloquy about hitting bottom and turning it over —as if we don't know.

When I mention we had to put Joshua out in below freezing weather, he says something about tough love. But living it is phenomenally more difficult than spouting theory. What do you do when they slam doors and fists into floors?

Or curse and yell and barrel through rooms or barricade themselves in three-day comas? Or take off for days without a note or a call? What do you do when you beg them to stay, but they have to go—you lock them out, but they show up desperate and desolate? What do you do when you hold their face in your hands and tell them how much they are loved, but it's still not enough? What to do when they slump in your arms, collapsed in despair? What do you do when they jump out the window and threaten suicide or sob at your feet? What do you do when they pace and pull at their hair, faces and voices twisted in terror? What do you do when their hearts turn to ice or shatter like glass before your pleading eyes? What do you do, just what do you do? Parents can show children love, but it doesn't guarantee they will love themselves.

My cousin doesn't get it. He proudly announces his thirteen-year-old son has never given them a moment's worry. I can't help but have to add—Joshua too had been a model child until that age. Not only does my cousin not get it, but neither does Joshua. While visiting him at rehab, he asks questions about his journey. He sits transfixed as I relate account after account of his downward spiral. Consequently, he requests excerpts from the journal to help strengthen his resolve. I hope he's prepared to look at the thief that stole his past.

Good to hear from Joshua again, but this time's a set-up. He says he wants to ask us something but is afraid. Friends from rehab invited him to the Science Center in Seattle and would we mind if he doesn't come home this weekend on his pass? Since he had promised to help with house repairs, I'm ticked but mostly worried. Why don't I wait before reacting? Like a forensic scientist I mustn't jump to conclusions but take it slow, a methodical walk-through wearing gloves and booties while grasping the big picture. I processed all night and now I'm feeling manipulated. Is he strategizing for a reunion with his pod and answering their whistle?

Just got off the phone and had a heart-to-heart with Joshua. We feel close again. Why can't I do this with friends? It never feels safe enough.

Spoke with my aunt this morning and mentioned Joshua seemed better. Her response, "Well, that's great Karla. Now when he gets out of there you have to keep him away from those friends." Shaking my head I answer, "We can't keep him from anything. We are completely powerless to control anyone but ourselves. We don't even have much influence anymore." It's exactly this kind of thinking that is distorted. But do I blame her? Not at all. Her intentions are good and motivation honorable.

Joshua got out on pass and went to court today and received the stiffest penalty so far—loss of his driver's license for a year. I'm down with a cold; I'm sure the stress has compromised my immune system. Try as I may, I did a lot wrong today. Instead of calling my sponsor, I dumped sadness and fear on Joshua. Tonight is the added guilt. I have so little faith in him. I have faith in God but so little trust and faith in my son. And neither does the court. The judge said its obvious Joshua remains a threat to public safety—therefore the license is suspended. Now he must work, survive and stay sober with this added burden. And the probation starts all over again—two years—or he goes to prison, not jail but prison. Prison must look good to Joshua: Three hots and a cot, hanging out with guys getting high (oh yes, prisons are full of drugs) maybe that's where he can be happy.

I want to see it in his eyes—to see the spiritual awakening—the tears, the humility, the *fear*. I call him on it and he defends himself accusing me of perfectionism, "I never do anything right—not even how I react to the judge's ruling." It's true. I never think he measures up to my ideal. He's never sorry enough, sad enough or serious enough. He never banishes the demons that snake under my skin. It's *my* faulty perceptions, not his shortcomings. How dare I judge his emotions and more importantly blame him for not taking care of mine.

*   *   *

The bear trap leaves me feeling old and unimportant. My sons are growing up. I feel awkward around them and their friends. I feel invisible. Once a woman of substance, now a mute shell, help out, pitch in and stay out of the way.

Their hugs are perfunctory and brief. My heart aches to feel special again. Must I buy their attention with servitude and silent compliance? Are my ideals lofty or rigid? I used to walk into a room and set it on fire. Now I'm a potted plant. My words are stilted, laughter forced and speech measured. How do I fit in? Where do I fit in?

When people see me, they see a dry husk. They don't see I'm a counselor, educator and accomplished public speaker. I once was a professional actress, singer and award-winning debater—once upon a time. Now I pass out napkins, change a diaper; scrub a pan.

*   *   *

While setting boundaries today, I was rude and hurtful. I haven't practiced long enough to take care of myself without taking it out on others. I'm ashamed and reluctant to set it aside. My penance will be an ever-greater attempt to make living amends. I'm so undeserving of God's grace and yet He blesses me everyday. His love makes me want to improve for Him.

Joshua is a week from departing rehab and the nervous jitters have arrived. We talk a good long talk about fears, trials and future challenges. He's scared, which is both good and bad. Good because he wasn't scared before, bad because this will be a daily battle. He's worried he will fail and is overwhelmed with starting again at ground zero. His fears are now my fears as hard as I try to let go. I comfort

80

him, "Joshua, if you relapse tomorrow or a thousand tomorrows, we will still love and believe in you. People recover and you can, too." Although fear is a companion, it does not paralyze me. He has as good a chance of making it this time as any. In "God's time" could mean this time.

* * *

Joshua gets out of rehab and we help him move into his recovery house in Seattle; buy a few groceries, help him settle in and now he's on his own. He has $70.00 in his pocket, a room, food, a bus pass and hopefully the resolve and God's grace to make it.

I'm at Al-Anon and meet a seventy-six-year-old woman. She's attending for the first time due to her forty-five- year-old heroin addict son. She has a restraining order against him and has spent close to $100,000 over the years. He is serving time in prison. My heart quivers when I hear her story. God, please don't let it be our story. It sweeps over cities where parents huddle in doorways hoping for the best, but knowing at any moment it can take their children.

Joshua calls from Seattle. He's overwhelmed and sounds stuffy from a stress cold. I reassure him it will fall into place. My friend's eighteen-year-old son is using again after fourteen months clean—on pot, crank, who knows? They're all in crisis. My heart aches for them, for us, for everyone adulterated by this disease.

A few days later Joshua's in a panic. His first words, "I didn't relapse," but his voice suggests brewing instability. Impulsively, he went to see a girl instead of continuing his job search, got stranded and missed an interview. He thanked me for positive words, not condemnation and called back this morning and said he found a job. Now the new stressor—can he keep it and stay clean? He reports it's harder every day. Imagine—harder not easier. And when he's tired the urge goes way, way up. Struggling only whets the appetite.

Jarred from deep sleep, Joshua calls a week later in the grip of cravings. Someone gave him concert tickets that were acting as a trigger. After a perfect day, money in his pocket, why not reward himself with a little controlled use? The insanity sneaks back with a gaggle of demons waiting in the wings. After nearly an hour on the phone, it's difficult to sleep and now this morning I'm hung over from the cluster pain. He wants to sell the concert tickets. Better to pour those energies into finding a meeting, but if I press or lecture I'm making him and me worse.

* * *

It's been several weeks and Joshua is clean, sober, working at a nice hotel, enrolled in college, going to meetings, church, calling home, friendly, happy, back! Ah, there is heaven right here on earth. Bob's business is booming and my job, wonderful. It has been said happiness isn't circumstance dependent—oh really? Joshua's exuberance is contagious. But I must remember falling coconuts kill 150 people each year. Danger can be deceptively disguised.

I call Joshua, and in the moment of a nice conversation ask, "So how many days clean do you have now, must be a lot, huh?" His response is disturbing, "Yeah, something like that." Then confesses to two slips—swears it was alcohol, so why is he sweating the next court-ordered U.A.? But what troubles me most is the suicidal ideation: "Mom, I felt like jumping out of an eleventh floor window. I would walk by and say, what's it all for?"

* * *

I haven't spoken to Joshua for a number of days, but we have communicated via phone messages. At first I did not grasp the significance. Is Joshua avoiding us? Is he relapsing? When we see him next, will I be able to tell one way or the other? Will he or I ever recover? Will the ideation return? Today is better than yesterday, but yesterday still keeps me from enjoying today.

I'm still so sick. I read into everything and let paranoia propel me into fatalistic thinking. Faulty perception colors and distorts. Like anyone under tyranny, suspicion is a brutal bully.

* * *

We spend Sunday with Jason and his wife and our grandson—church, zoo and a nice lunch overlooking the Sound. But returning home, there's an urgent message from Joshua and we can't reach him. I must remind myself things can change in an instant just as easily from bad to good, and prepare myself to act rather than react. I do hope it's nothing serious. The phone rings. It is a collect call. I take it. He's relapsed on alcohol. I feel agitated but no tears. Just two months out of rehab and no longer a slip but a full-blown relapse. What now? What next? A ghostly wind whistles.

When the doorbell rings at 11:00 P.M, I should know its Joshua in bad shape. There he is on our front porch, and my first thought, he's been kicked out of his halfway house and lost his job. Well, not yet. He played hooky—set himself up to use crank and came very close. As he broke down, we prayed for his strength and release. He explained he's in a parallel universe. He hates it when he uses, but constantly wants to use, so hates it when he's not using. How this disease gets us into fear. How it steamrolls us time and again.

Nonetheless, Bob and I are getting better. We're not only going and doing more but enjoying it when we do with other thoughts, dreams even concerns unrelated to Joshua.

We have fun playing and kidding. Like this morning, when Bob stepped out of the shower before grabbing a towel and says, "Your last chance to look before everything's covered up," and then later, when we're having a friendly little squabble about leftover dessert I ask, "Are you going to eat the last of your cupcakes?"

"Yes," he answers. "And you've already had yours."

"I know...but can I have one more?" I say, smiling and batting my lashes.

"Have this," Bob chuckles and grabs his crotch.

"I have standards," I say, flipping my hair and playing along with indignation. "I won't prostitute myself for a cupcake."

"How 'bout two?" he offers, and we both break up laughing. Life's better, when just days ago we were sitting in dirt with our hand out.

* * *

When we first moved to the northwest, I fought moss from creeping into our flowerbeds. I would scrape and dig and poison and pull it up by huge clumps only to have it grow back thicker and deeper the next time. It was a battle that could not be won. Finally I gave up. I surrendered to the moss and let it invade and wander when and where it would. At first I could not bear to look at it.

But that was then and this is now. Today, my beds are covered in lush, emerald moss and dotted here and there flowers burst from a blanket of velvet. And best of all, I never dig or hoe because it's breathtaking. Once I accepted the moss and its lust for unregulated growth, neglect became an ally. It was allowed to meet its destiny and proved itself a worthy warrior. Once despised, it evolved into a thing of surprising beauty. Once I turned it over, it was allowed to be all it was intended. Could it be my son's disease will produce something as wonderful? Just like the moss, I will wait for the shoots to stretch and dazzle.

However it appears the wait will be long; Joshua relapses again and heads back into the unfaithful disease. Nothing comes as a surprise. Is this recovery? Addiction tells him he has many trials before it catches him. The disease lies.

I take a risk and reveal to a not-so-close friend I am feeling lonely. I think she's surprised I'm open and vulnerable. People tell me I look together—if only they knew. I heard it explained that self-pity is when you think you're sucked under roiling water, but really bobbing for sympathy. To quell my fears I call Joshua, but he doesn't answer. Questions flutter in my head. Is he full of shame and needs to avoid us? Is he in jail and in such despair he cannot face us? Or has he been thrown out of his apartment, lost his job or both?

At bedtime I thank God for whatever is happening, has happened or will happen. And today, I learned what happened. He had to work overtime. None of the fears ensued, in fact, a blessing took place. Joshua took up the slack caused by a no-show. Others had to rearrange schedules because someone chose an irresponsible act that propelled the shift of events. Joshua had often been that irresponsible someone. Now he was looking at it from the other side and better understood the impact of his disease-driven selfish acts, his no-shows, walk-offs or firings.

*　*　*

Joshua's back on track and like a tulip in a garden window, I've opened to the sun. Is that because I'm doing better or because he is? Next time I hope if I can't give Joshua the benefit of the doubt, I can remember to give it to God.

Easing back into the flow we have a successful dinner party. I'm nervous but not too rusty. Everybody has a good time, although one couple has to leave early because the husband's fourteen-year-old son comes home to his mom's house drunk and disorderly. I don't disclose Joshua's story but perhaps some day I will. I don't have to tell everyone, everything, every time.

But the disease reminds me happiness is transient. I visit Joshua and he describes the daily struggle that threatens serenity. He looks healthy, but it must be similar for a family waiting from check-up to check-up to see if the cancer has returned. Vigilance prepares and protects me.

I drive away and cry for two reasons: First, because of the joy I see in him. Second, because this loving soul is stalked day and night by an unrelenting monster.

FOUR

Blame Pain

Timeless

Researchers have discovered light breaks its own speed limit, which crumbles the deeply held notion of causality—that the cause of something always precedes its effects. Parent pain is partly self-induced. Participatory pain requires cooperation. I have crucified myself thinking I caused Joshua to become an addict because it happened on my watch. But it's my best guess even if it had happened long after he grew up and moved out I still would have flogged myself. But now it's time to starve the shame with facts and other possibilities: Addicts answer siren calls.

Many believe families have the greatest influence on children. Kids aren't robots or androids. But parents, who provide good role models, are lumped together with parents who fall short. Parents *may* make a difference, but the operative word is *may*, not *can*. No one can make anyone do anything regardless of well-found intentions or the closest, loving ties.

Since the boys were babies, I read to them, talked to them, educated and informed them. I got on my knees and begged them never to start and to stop when they did. But, they are going to do whatever they want to do, and nothing, I repeat, nothing else matters. I know, they know and God knows we were good parents —it was the luck of the draw that our kid, your kid, are risk-takers and not cautious and compliant. They carry genes, which make them think, feel and react differently. They carry the gene for addiction, and it is a powerful blueprint. The call is great, and they are *programmed* to answer it.

To all those who blame parents: This exacts horrendous suffering in a silent segment of society. Yes, there are neglectful, self-centered parents who are too busy, disinterested or sick to guide, direct and properly parent children, but please give other ones benefit of the doubt and their rightful credit. Some children become addicted and others not. Parents who have firsthand experience subvert the collectively held opinion, but everywhere accusations and pointed fingers scream out from billboards, newspapers, radio, TV and film...from religious pulpits and political grandstands...from bumper stickers to the man on the street.

QUIPS AND QUOTES

"Parents: The Anti Drug." "Talk to your kids about drugs, about smoking—they'll listen!" KIRO, Channel 7, TV Commercial, November 5, 1999.

"Dare to keep kids off drugs." Dare Bumper Sticker.

"Parents who get involved in their children's activities raise kids who are less likely to use drugs. Get the book on raising a drug-free child." Office of National Drug Control Policy.

"Hugs, not drugs." Slogan on a shopping bag.

"That's what we owe our children—to give them the strength to say 'no,' to give them the character and confidence. It begins in the home with good role models to live by." Gen. Colin Powell, Republican National Convention, Philadelphia, Pa. August 2000.

"A little time—A BIG DIFFERENCE." Billboard ad picture of father with child.

"A lot of time, NO DIFFERENCE!" Bob's rebuttal under his breath.

"When you were a child was there someone who read to you? Took you to a museum, zoo and concert? Told you not to smoke and do drugs?" Gen. Colin Powell—TV Advertisement.

"I can keep a kid off drugs." TV commercial, close up of a woman, facing the camera, confident, shaming and proclaiming her power.

"If you bungle raising your children, then nothing else really matters."
Jackie Onassis (John F. Kennedy Jr. smoked enough pot to turn that gloat fest on its ear.)

"The enforcer, she's more than a hero, she's a good mom. When I say no weed, I mean no weed. You're more powerful than you know." TV advertisement December 16, 2003, Discovery Channel. (My rebuttal: **"You're less powerful than you think."**)

I wonder what Carrol O'Connor, Paul Newman, Bill Moyers, Barbara Eden and Senator George McGovern think about these statements since they are among the many unfortunate who lost children to alcohol-drug addictions.

The shame of addiction is greater than stupidity. Many times I have been a walking, talking corpse, functioning on little sleep for days; slow, forgetful, difficulty tracking, attending, relating, missing points, jokes, innuendo and *too ashamed* to defend myself when snickers, asides and eyes roll with judgment or derision. Better to be a fool, stupid, menopausal or inept, than *God forbid,* the mother of an addict worried out of her mind. Better to be losing one's mind than to be shamed and stigmatized by this disease, a disease that might hurt *you.* My son might run *you* over, might rob or rip *you* off to get a buck. And wouldn't you hate me just a little? I gave birth to this pariah, and if you're unacquainted with the disease, might you think somehow I helped create the wretch? Doesn't every D.A.R.E. challenge point a finger? D.A.R.E. TO KEEP KIDS OFF DRUGS. The toxic shame and social stigma catapult you into arenas that set you up, strip you down and bare a false self. What's the definition of manslaughter? Addiction.

"DADS GO 'AWOL' IN ANTI DRUG WAR SURVEY; aloof fathers seem to raise chances that kids will abuse substances." Edward Walsh, Washington Post.

There it is again, blame, blame and more blame. Edward Walsh says, "A relative lack of paternal involvement is key in determining whether teenagers begin to use drugs."

How excruciating to read this indictment and see the pain scorched onto my husband's face—a man so loving and devoted and now wrongly accused as a bad father. Studies are skewed. No doubt there is a link with acting-out and dysfunctional homes, but how does one account for addiction striking loving, devoted families? How does one explain *that* away? Just could it be this is truly a disease no one causes?

What good does this do to eradicate the scourge? Is it reasonable to expect uninvolved fathers will take the time to make a permanent, positive change? And what does it do to the nurturing and invested fathers whose hearts are already broken? These dads did not cause or condone. They supported, disciplined, followed up and followed through. They cuddled and tickled, tackled and tucked in and read to and prayed with and cried for again and again and again. These fathers do exist and still have children who try that first taste of alcohol, puff a cigarette or smoke a joint. These great dads have great kids who make great mistakes. Even when admonished and warned, some kids try it the first time. And for those who are *real* addicts, the switch flips and the disease activates. A disease, explained to us, that doesn't say, yeah, try a little now, maybe more later, but stop in order for school tomorrow, football practice or Thanksgiving dinner. No, a disease that screams, "FEED ME, FEED ME!" And then whispers in their ear and deceives them into a dream, which evolves into a night terror without end. A disease that heaps enormous guilt on the good kids from the good families with the good parents because it only confirms this kid, this poor addicted kid, must be fundamentally flawed. How else can one explain they would do what they do and hurt the parents they love so deeply? And with that pain the cravings grow stronger and the pattern well entrenched, leaving another family in the gullet of the gargoyle. Remember, a smidgeon of liquor on a scorpion's back will make it instantly go mad and sting itself to death.

Good, happy kids, from good, loving homes, pick up the first time not from pain or abandonment but from sheer curiosity and biological drive. The question is how do we tame a genetic monster? Perhaps someday a simple blood test can reveal which babies carry the gene for addiction and vaccines and gene therapy will be the anti-drug. But until then, parents deal with critical ablation.

TEEN STUDY: A REMINDER COMMUNICATION IS KEY:

Researchers from the University of Minnesota and the University of North Carolina—Chapel Hill, indicate teenagers are far less likely to smoke, drink alcohol, become sexually active, or engage in other disruptive and potentially destructive behavior if they enjoy strong emotional attachments to key adults in their lives, primarily parents and teachers. TACOMA NEWS TRIBUNE, September 15, 1997

"Teens who join sports teams are more likely to be clean-cut and less likely to use drugs, smoke, have sex..." Archives of Pediatrics & Adolescent Medicine, published by the American Medical Association. TACOMA NEWS TRIBUNE, September 15, 2000

Joshua was captain of his summer soccer team in elementary school. He came in first in his division in an elementary running club. He was first-string varsity football in middle school and lettered and made first-string high school varsity football as a sophomore.

"ASKING QUESTIONS: THE ANTI-DRUG.
Parents, it isn't pestering, it's good parenting." TV advertisement

Who, what, when, where? We checked. We followed. We even spied. We begged, pleaded, warned and questioned. We had family meetings and nightly family dinners. I was a stay-at-home mom until Joshua was nine, and then only worked part-time and was home after school. I volunteered for the PTA and Scouts, took them to church, Sunday school, summer camp, vacations, museums and libraries. We loved, cherished and cared. We often made them angry and were accused of being hard-nosed and nosy. But none of it mattered. In spite of our best efforts, both of our sons tried alcohol and drugs, and Joshua became an addict. Granted, they're good, compassionate young men, and maybe we helped contribute, but I don't know for sure. We are their parents and it was our job to keep them safe. We were mandated to teach and guide them, to reach and inspire them. But moms and dads can only do so much. Parents cannot be with their children every second.

I heard about a young woman who worked as a manager for a fast food restaurant and described her parents as knowing her whereabouts every minute of the day until she was married.

She was furious following a terrifying experience when she, along with two teenage employees, were gagged and bound following a robbery. She and the girls spent the night tied up on the floor and were discovered by other employees the next morning. Expecting the girls' parents to arrive after closing time, she was incensed when they never came looking for their daughters. The manager went on to say she actually felt more anger at the parents than the men who robbed them...going on to ask the rhetorical question: What kind of parent is unaware their teenage daughter is gone all night? She described the girls as fine teenagers, but with parents who are irresponsible.

Again and again people blame parents. First, to the manager: I seriously doubt your parents knew your whereabouts *every* minute of the day until you were married. If so, that sounds like an exaggeration and if it were possible, highly suspect. That kind of control speaks volumes about dysfunctional enmeshment.

Now, as to why the parents did not call or come to the restaurant, I offer some ideas: It is quite possible the girls may have told their parents they would be spending the night with friends after work. Why would the parents be alarmed? They did not expect them to come home. Now you might ask, if they were planning sleepovers, wouldn't their friends have called the parents when they didn't show? Unlikely. Friends cover for friends. And why would parents of good kids expect anything amiss?

Maybe these fine teenagers are fine actresses, and if they are adept at pulling the wool over their parents' eyes, they could surely put one over on you with their public personas. Would it occur to most parents the restaurant was robbed? If they had driven to the site would anything have looked out of place? What if their daughters had gotten a ride there and were being picked up later?

Maybe these parents called all of their daughters' friends and parents and maybe they knew there had to be a good explanation because, after all, their daughters are fine teenagers. Maybe they knew police would not initiate a search until they had been missing for forty-eight hours. But, maybe they walked the floors worried out of their minds. Maybe these girls told their parents they were sleeping over at each other's houses and as fine teenagers, they wouldn't have raised their parents' suspicions.

And lastly, maybe these parents suspected the kids were up to no good but felt utterly powerless. Since the girls were thirteen or fourteen they had been out of control. When grounded they would kick, scream, break things, jump out windows, run away and threaten suicide...but publicly, look and act like fine teenagers.

Maybe it wasn't the first time this happened, and what were the parents to do? Lock them to a post, beat and starve them? Realistically, what, just what can a parent do short of having them arrested, emancipated as minors or put in foster homes or psyche wards? Parents, heart-sick and paralyzed, are reduced to ineffective bystanders.

Maybe these fine girls get straight A's, but do crank and drink like fish——but it's early in their disease and so far no one has a clue. They are manipulative and charming and in their parents' confusion, easily dance circles around them.

And maybe these parents *were* neglectful, permissive losers—but then how did they have these fine teenagers? Maybe you, the manager, need to work through your pain. What you endured is terrible, but so is parent pain just as real and culpability misplaced.

Most parents don't know their kids are using, a few don't care and are getting high with them, but the majority are paralyzed by clandestine suffering. Will addicts get to heaven? Will their parents? I sure hope so, because they have already spent long enough in hell.

A Note On The Inside Cover Of Joshua's Bible From A Friend, An Anonymous Addict:

"To Josh, I know it may be a very <u>long time</u> before you read this, but I thank you for letting me stay at your place. Thanks for sharing your clothes with me when I had none. Thanks for sharing your last bite of food when there was nothing in the house to eat. God knows what you have done. He sees through your heart, and He will Bless you a thousand fold."

Parenting was consecrated time—sacred, special and elevated in precedence. But ready or not, it was ripped out from under us. Because addicts are maligned, parents automatically are guilty by association. The war on drugs has dissolved into finger pointing that leaves doors open for blame and zero solutions.

Last night I passed the same church I see every day. On the reader board, there's always a catchy little phrase, but unlike many in the past that were clever and supportive, this one infuriated and wounded.

"Parents who are plugged into their kids rarely get shocked." I felt compelled to respond:

To Whom It May Concern,

I live in your neighborhood and frequently pass your church. Over the years I have enjoyed many of the messages displayed on the reader board. But the current phrase wounds. I'm sure the intention is a wake-up call to parents who are pre-occupied, neglectful or disinterested in their children. But please let me illuminate what the message means to me.

I am a parent of a wonderful son who was raised in a loving and devoted family. We moved to Puyallup because of the schools and tranquil setting.

In spite of being very "plugged into" our son, we were shocked to learn he was using drugs. And also

95

shocked to learn Pierce County is second only to San Diego as the meth capital of the western United States and Washington State has the dubious distinction of being third in the nation following Missouri and California for the most meth labs, Pierce County, leading all counties in western United States for meth labs. There are 1.9 million teens that use meth in this country.

Our son was an honor student, star athlete, loved, cherished and grew up with Christian values. Today he is a full-blown crank addict. This disease strikes all families and does not discriminate. There is a myth that must be dispelled: No one causes this disease! It is a disease that is cunning, baffling and powerful, and no one really knows why some fall victim, any more than we understand why children contract leukemia. Yes, some neglected, angry, troubled kids turn to drugs, but some kids turn to drugs out of curiosity and a genetic predisposition. One thing we know is certain: We have met many loving, wonderful, "plugged in parents" who all got the shocks of their lives. Parents who are held accountable for their children's disease are as much victims of this plague as their disabled children. Please give beleaguered parents the benefit of doubt.

What keeps us going is the Word, "Raise them up in the way of the Lord, and when they are old they will not depart from it." We cling to that promise, that one day, when he is mature, he will recover.

I venture a guess we're not the only parents in pain who drive by your church. What words of comfort can you offer instead of indictment? Parents affected by their children's disease need compassion and support, rather than accusations in the court of public opinion and most of all, houses of worship.

A Parent in Pain

Eagerly I watch for the reply or will it be a rebuttal? Will it be comforting, compassionate or accusatory?

There it is on the reader board:

"More prayers might get answered, if more prayers are prayed."

Great, another sinister minister shaming those branded by the beast; I might have known. We're not praying enough. We're not doing enough. And we pray *all* the time.

How much I wanted to see and read something like the following:

"God will not fail you." "He keeps His word; He keeps His promises." "Rest in the assurance, He is in control." "Do not be dismayed, He is with you."

"It is important for parents to inform kids that drugs are harmful, unacceptable and will not be tolerated. Know what your children are doing. Know who they hang with; make arrangements for them to participate in supervised after-school activities." Edward Jurich, Acting Director, Office of National Drug Control Policy, Washington, D.C.

How absurd, an acting director who knows so little about the disease. Let's look at each of these separately:

1. <u>KNOW WHAT YOUR CHILDREN ARE DOING</u>: Parents can't know what their children are doing every minute. When parents drop kids at a mall, movie or county fair, unless the parents follow, spy and escort, it's impossible. Many kids use their first drug, alcohol, during daylight hours in the safety of school and private homes.

2. <u>KNOW WHO THEY HANG WITH</u>: Kids can walk out the front door with their best parent-approved friends and meet Tom, Dick or Kerri anywhere, anytime, unless the parents have them leashed. Yes, when they spend the night,

97

parents can speak directly to the other parents, but there may still be ample opportunity to sneak out and go to an impromptu party. For instance, one evening when Joshua was fifteen and grounded, the house alarm was set even though we were home. We heard a signal the front door was opening. As we investigated, Joshua wasn't sneaking out (although he had jumped from his second floor window and done that before) but a thirteen-year-old neighbor girl was sneaking in. It was one o'clock in the morning. She had walked five blocks in the dark alone while her parents slept at *her* house. When I called them, at first they politely said I was mistaken—there was no way their daughter had done this, as she was fast asleep upstairs in her warm and safe bed. She had never led them to believe she was capable of such an impulsive and reckless act.

So what did they do? They grounded her, lectured, loved and reasoned, as they cared deeply and were very hands-on. She was an honor student and accomplished gymnast. They sought professional help, but in spite of every effort, this lovely girl with good parents went on and became an addict and had a child out of wedlock. This girl was destined to live on the edge—destined and driven by her brain, the command center for the disease.

3. <u>MAKE ARRANGEMENTS FOR THEM TO PARTICIPATE IN SUPERVISED AFTER-SCHOOL ACTIVITIES</u>: Joshua and Jason were in Scouts, sports, church youth groups; we went camping, fishing, boating, family outings to museums and points of interest. We did *everything* "hands-on parents" are supposed to do and so did the other family. Hands-on parenting does not prevent addiction any more than it prevents leukemia.

As this girl's disease progressed, these parents—heartsick and terrified—had her swooped up and sent to a $25,000 in-patient treatment center in another state. In the middle of the night two men "escorted" their daughter and put her on a plane. She came out three months later and quickly relapsed. I saw the mom one day and asked how it was going. With blank eyes she said, "We're living in hell." Nodding and barely moving my lips I replied, "I know...I know."

How dare you blame these broken souls? How dare you pass judgment and dismiss us with the wave of your judgmental and presumptuous hand. Save your breath and dollars and find a real cure, a real prevention for this murderous monster.

And for you very "hands-on" parents who check, control, re-check, follow, spy, sneak, investigate, doubt, bend over backwards and forwards and proudly pat yourselves on the back as your children trot to college having never been in trouble—just how confident are you that these kids, these kids who have never tasted freedom, won't succumb to the titillating temptations that await them? What tools will they have in the real world? Oh, don't worry—if they don't carry the gene for addiction, they'll do you proud. They may drink or even drug, but function all the same and graduate and zoom forward as you strut your righteous stuff. But if, just if, old Uncle Joe, the drunk from way back when, passed his defective little gene along to Susie-Q or Johnny Blue—honey hold onto your heart because you're in for one soul-crushing ride. You've just entered your worst nightmare that will shred your life and laugh with demonic glee.

So there it is, an easy deduction: bad parents raise bad kids. Society still believes kids on drugs must have been screwed up by the parental unit. Some say kids use drugs because they are sad, mad, bad, hurt or misled...ignored or rejected, abused or neglected. But I can only tell our story. Joshua says he and he alone felt different from the start. With steely eyes staring, he reports he *always* knew he'd be an addict; he knew it before he ever drank alcohol, smoked grass, did shrooms, did crank. He knew it when he was thirteen pretending to do a line. He knew it, wanted it and pursued, sought, found and became what he was drawn to from that deep calling within his DNA. He knew he was born to do this. He knew, like Robert Downey Jr., the actor knew, that premonition of self-destruction, that early notion he was born with a gene for reckless self-implosion.

Sooner or later they will find a way to satisfy their destiny. Drugs are the granddaddy of all roller coasters. Threading the needle, addicts push the boundaries and recreational use burnishes heredity from a small ember to a raging inferno. Like drugs, chemical dependents burn fast and furious.

Question of the day:
Is addiction the result of dysfunction or does addiction cause dysfunction?

Many blame parents, but experts know this disease is more powerful than anyone. Addicts' brains are different; therefore drugs feel extra special, sweeter than any nectar drawing them to evil. Because endorphin systems burn out, addicts are unable to tolerate even nominal discomfort. In addition to biology, addicts build up years of difficult consequences because the disease is a human wrecking ball. Left with shame, guilt and multiple losses, the floodgate opens to cravings more intense than any normal person can imagine. Once the switch is thrown, the disease demands to be quenched. All perceptions are filtered through this poison prism and the compromised brain, a brain that believes it *cannot* live without chemicals.

But addicts also share personality traits. They avoid uncomfortable feelings. These feelings range from traumas to waiting in line at the grocery store. Chemical dependents retreat from discomfort, especially honesty that leads to pain, even necessary pain that leads to growth. The irony: The avoidance of pain creates greater pain, proving there are no shortcuts. Life demands full payment from each of us—but also rewards with real see-it, feel-it and know-it truths. Can addicts be identified in the cradle? Are these the babies who can't entertain themselves when they awake? That was Joshua.

Could it be addicts differ from norms not only on a biochemical level, but also in terms of temperament, ability to experience life, satisfaction and discernment? Once mind-altering drugs are chronically ingested the pleasure receptors in the brain are damaged. But perhaps the brains of addicts are *already* genetically altered prior to their first experimentation. They are compelled to seek and find that which satiates the unseen force from within. But how can this clinically be proven? Were it possible to find a Rosetta stone, could we then formulate gene therapy for embryos in utero? For its evident, even under the best of circumstances, some infants grow up, experiment and become addicted. It's only a matter of time.

If this explains addiction, can we then stop blaming ourselves? Haven't your children told you it wasn't your fault? That you didn't cause it? That it was their destiny and theirs alone? Start believing them and loose that albatross about your neck. And if they do blame you, you don't have to believe it. All parents make mistakes—some great, some small, *but those mistakes do not cause addictions*.

This disease is an amalgamation of superstition, paranoia and genetic personification. It's idiopathic because science cannot explain what causes it and society blames and condemns parents because it fears what it cannot understand.

Therefore, can we extrapolate genetics loads the gun, but environment pulls the trigger? Remember, not so long ago parents were blamed for schizophrenia, autism and even dyslexia. Like then and now, public sentiment is based on ignorance and a desire to explain the unexplainable. The mandate is clear: Parents do your job and your children are unlikely to use alcohol and drugs. And if they should use, abuse and become addicted, it's also your job to fix them.

What's the solution? Choose your partner well? Look to genetic markers? Hold your breath and cross your fingers?

"Parents, you don't know! You have no idea! Your kids have a whole secret life you know nothing about. Don't matter what kinda parents—kids are gonna do what they do." Sinbad, Comedian, Paramount Theater—Seattle, Washington—February 3, 2001

"As far as my family and the life I had, that wasn't why I was drinking. I was drinking because I was an alcoholic." Dennis Hopper, actor/director

"No parent should have to compete with popular culture to raise their children." Joseph Lieberman, Democratic V.P. Candidate at the Democratic Convention

"A study suggests that thrill/risk taking behaviors are associated with a gene that causes a lessening release of dopamine in the brain of addictive individuals and people who engage in high-risk endeavor." KIRO TV, Channel 7 News

"Our youths now love luxury. They have bad manners, contempt for authority; they show disrespect for their elders, and love chatter in places of exercise. They no longer rise when elders enter the room. They contradict their parents, chatter before company, gobble up their food and tyrannize their teachers." Socrates, 5th Century, B.C. (Did they also abuse chemicals?)

Some believe addiction is a personal failure—a character defect first manifested in parents and then perpetrated on children. This exonerates science and stigmatizes families. But, we parents of addicts by no means have the market cornered on pain. My daughter-in-law's parents are selling their house. They have an interested buyer who loves it, but has reservations. The property is quite appealing except it sits on a traditional street surrounded by other nice homes.

This buyer's family has two children, one with autism, and the other with Tourette's syndrome, a neurological condition that causes erratic movement and sudden and unexpected vocal outbursts. This family fears condemnation from neighbors. They are willing to forgo their favorite house to ensure isolation from public scorn. No doubt their pain shapes their decisions both great and small. And yet, only the most uninformed would dare hold these parents responsible for their children's disabilities.

Parents of addicts and alcoholics don't deserve to be maligned. Some kids have an affinity to gravitate to the edge. I'm reminded of what I heard at a meeting, "They tumble down ever path you warn."

*   *   *

What dark forces lurk in the great out there? Like the Garden of Eden, surrounded with abundance and armed with warnings, Eve ate the apple and Adam followed. They had it good and yet they were dissatisfied. Was it Satan or were they the first addictive personalities? Satan is the great seducer: "Oh come on, nobody will know…" and Satan is the great accuser: "Forget about treatment and meetings. You're a piece of crap; you'll never get out of this."

As Stephen Hill, a recovering addict and now nationally recognized evangelist who led nightly revival services in Pensacola, Florida, writes in, *Charisma*, March 1998:

"At first my conscience had bothered me, but after awhile, misbehaving became natural. Instead of being guided by my parents' teachings, I began yielding to the inner voice that always encouraged me to give in to my own selfish desires. The voice of selfish evil convinced me that he was my friend, the one to lead and guide me. My parents constantly tried to correct me...I was becoming very adept at disobeying. The evil voice echoed inside me, 'It's a whole new world. Everybody is doing drugs! They won't hurt you.' My parents and teachers had clearly warned me against drug and alcohol abuse. But between my rebellion, peers, and the voice of my 'guide,' I was hooked...I felt drugs could temporarily eradicate the guilt I felt from doing what I knew was wrong..."

Since they were babies, I read to my children every day and every night. Once they could read themselves, we also included family reading nights a couple of evenings a week. I brought home bags full of library books and read them from cover to cover. I did this because I wanted to introduce good literature and foster a love for books. I love to read but Joshua does not. In spite of every good effort he never picks up a book, darkens a bookstore or visits a library.

You can instruct, inform, admonish and warn, but they're going to do what they're going to do. Can you feel my frustration as you read these lines? Or when you listen to my song, *What They Do*?

I saw a magazine layout that caught my eye and soothed my soul. Pictured from head to foot was a young man standing with his hands in his pockets and a smirk on his unshaven face. His hair was a dirty, spiked mop, his ears looked pierced and his clothes were more grunge than hip. In the top left-hand corner of the photo was one word, son* and below, listed as if on a recipe card, were the following:

1   y-chromosome
1200   diapers
9 variations of peek-a-boo
1   set of encyclopedias
43 ½ hours helping with science projects
1   meaningful conversation per week
20 feet of space when near his friends
100,000 dollars for college

Shape ingredients into responsible adult. May not adhere to mold. Remove when finished or charge rent. *Results may vary, McCall's – May 2000

Everyone wants to know what causes someone to become an addict. I don't have the answers, only questions and our personal story. Is addiction the result of cross-pollination of risky behavior and risk-loving character? Is it genetic determinism? Or is it just all the parents' fault?

To those hit and run zealots who judge and condemn, may your future never betray a promising past or as a guy once said when someone dented his car, "Go forth and multiply," but not exactly in those same words. Life is full of simple pleasures—licking the bowl, rocking on a porch swing, extracting the perfect revenge. Tugged and taut, it's best when pulled complete and unwilling.

KARLA KLEAR SKY'S BUMPER STICKERS

ADDICTION IS A DISEASE NOT A CHOICE	SCIENCE NOT PARENTS: THE ANTI-DRUG
ADDICTION: PARENTS DON'T CAUSE IT, CAN'T CONTROL IT, CAN'T CURE IT	ADDICTION: GENES OF MASS DESTRUCTION
ADDICTION: TREATMENT BEFORE INCARCERATION	ADDICTION: HEREDITY NOT NEGLECT OR ABUSE
ADDICTION: JUST SAYING NO DOESN'T STOP A DISEASE	ADDICTION: DARE TO ADMIT IT COULD HAPPEN TO YOU
ADDICTION: A BRAIN DISEASE NOT MORAL TURPITUDE	ADDICTS: A DISEASE IN PROGRESS
ADDICTS: CAN RECOVER, PARENTS CAN SURVIVE AND THRIVE	ADDICTION: PARENT PAIN DO YOU BLAME AND SHAME?
ADDICTS: GOOD PEOPLE WITH A BAD DISEASE	ADDICTION: GOOD PARENTS CAN HAVE GOOD ADDICTS WITH BAD DISEASES
ADDICTION: A DARK HOLE OF SHAME AND BLAME	ADDICTION LIKE BRAIN TUMORS DON'T RESPOND TO WARNINGS
ADDICTION: DON'T POINT A FINGER, OFFER A HAND	ADDICTION VACCINE: THE ANTI DRUG
PARENTING: A CRAP SHOOT REGARDLESS OF STRATEGY	ADDICTION: FREE PARENTS IN PAIN. COMPASSION NOT SHAME
ADDICTION: THE PLAGUE OF THE 21ST CENTURY	ADDICTION POINTS FINGERS AND SUCKS SOULS

FIVE

Pain & Promise
1999

Reflecting on the past years, the last couple in particular, how far have we come and what has it cost? It has cost us dearly. Two years ago Joshua was fresh out of his first in-patient, fresh out of jail and as we prepared for Jason's wedding, we had a back-up best man just in case. Two years ago, sick with despair, each day was a test of survival to make it to the next. Sleep-deprived and suffering, I slipped further into the abyss and found fault with everyone and everything. Hypersensitive, I wore martyrdom like a badge and depression was a constant companion. A co-dependent savant, I was so good my hand was Velcroed to my forehead. I sabotaged and blew up most relationships as a way of escape so I no longer faced what I once was and had now become.

We were all out of our minds, the disease taking huge chunks. But now, two years later, we are recovering, albeit with heavy losses. Joshua has worked steadily for close to six months, is living in a half-way house and we're all working our programs.

Bob and I are also singing again after a thirty-year hiatus. We met in 1967 when I auditioned as lead singer in his rock band. Music is a mutual and treasured passion. Our lives are improving, as is our self worth. But life is life with daily challenges.

Joshua phoned with disappointing news—his application was rejected so he won't be getting a better apartment. Also, a girl stood him up on a date, so it was a bad day. Ironically, he says bad days are less of a trigger than great ones. I suggested maybe that's why God didn't allow everything to work out.

I feel uneasy but can't put my finger on it. I fight unproductive, self-abasing thoughts; the carry-over is shaken confidence and lowered self-esteem. Last night at Al-Anon, I was painfully aware of how shallow and boring I've become. I don't know what to say or how to say it. I'm dour and unapproachable. What ever happened to the natural flow and ease? What happened to me? Do you wear a sign? *"Been beat up, not much left—treat with care or don't approach."* People used to belong to bridge groups, now they belong to support groups. Both serve similar purposes: They sit at tables and discuss the cards dealt to them.

* * *

To live well is to grieve well. What some call martyrdom I call meaningful misery, important and essential: The permission to feel fully, grieve completely and mourn that, which needs to be mourned, that which is purged with swollen anticipation. Wallowing in self-pity isn't necessarily bad. A mud bath is soothing and after the clay is rinsed, one feels better. While in pain, we have a right to go through it, but we must eventually move through and out of it.

When I was ten years old my finger was accidentally smashed in a car door. The immediate pain was so intense I rocked back and forth and screamed in agony. The after-pain however, came in pulsing throbs culminating days later in urgent pleas for relief. Mom, desperate to alleviate the suffering, takes me to the nearest doctor.

Although curled next to mother, I am fearful as I sit in the unfamiliar lobby waiting to have my finger examined. Everything is different about this place, a medical office sandwiched in the middle of a quiet, residential neighborhood. It looks like most of the large, vintage, three-stories on the street, except for the small brass placard on the door. The waiting room, only vaguely disguised, still reflects the grandeur of the fine living room it had once been—tall ceiling, polished oak floor, windows with sashes and a fireplace in one corner flanked by painted bookshelves enclosed with beveled glass and fancy pulls.

The courteous nurse ushers me alone into the doctor's private office, not examining room, where I wait for what will happen next; longing for Mom but too big to ask. The old doctor, stern and silent, leans forward, looks at the swollen, throbbing finger and takes a large paper clip from the drawer of his huge mahogany desk. He unfolds the clip and when it's unbent, with one stretched wire facing out, he flicks a lighter and holds the flame to the metal until it glows red-hot. My eyes are focused saucers. Here I am, a little girl in a strange place, in the hands of a very strange man.

"Put your finger out," he orders, and I do what is commanded. Slowly, with the precision of a surgeon, he holds the blazing clip to the top of the bulging nail. With pressure and gradual force, it burns through until a gusher of pus, blood and fetid stench oozes onto the gauze pad.

More fascinated than fearful, the relief is instantaneous and the process short and complete. Although the nail eventually turned purple-black and slowly loosened and lifted from the bed, the throbbing never returned and the healing began. The nail grew once again, albeit slightly deformed, but stronger and harder than the rest.

Pain is a signal you haven't gotten it all out. Don't be misguided or shamed by labeling your *necessary* ventilation as weak whining, but rather the natural order of things—a course of healing the squalid residue of a battle-strewn beach with your soul mired in the misfortune of disease, a disease that smashes your soul not once but over and over again with the intensity of a thousand howitzers bombing Normandy.

I've always been a harsh critic, reluctant to grant clemency to self or others. This perfectionism is born of deep-seated insecurities awash in shame. Joshua scrapes by with bravado, not to mention a merciful God hovering in the wings. I've been good at many things, which makes me supremely over-confident I can fix him, but this foolish pride leads to a paradigm shift, which alters perception.

Life fills up humility with accidental accoutrements. Yesterday, while strolling Freight House Square, I strike up a conversation with a radio talk-show hostess who broadcasts live interviews from the small shopping center. As I chat with her, I mention I am writing a book. She inquires what it is called and wants to know more, but first asks what, if any qualifications I have to write it. I reply, "I'm the mother of a meth addict."

The conversation brings an invitation to be a guest on her show, but I don't feel ready. For the time being I will ponder the risk. I hope this isn't a missed opportunity but a sign to continue my quest. When people are at the limits of survival, they need a tender ally.

Joshua hasn't felt well for over three weeks with pain in his legs. Tomorrow another doctor's visit, more tests, more waiting. I pray he receives an accurate and manageable diagnosis. Like a tot tugging a sleeve, fear has hold of me tonight. Just as Joshua is making progress, another detour, another interruption in this newfound peace. It's discouraging. Only eight months of relative normalcy and it's back to gripping scenarios that whittle hope. Someone asks, "Haven't we had our quota of pain? When will happiness stop being rationed in teaspoons?" Bob just got a call from an old friend. I answered, but was preoccupied and hope he didn't feel offended. I'm so distracted, so unavailable for anyone, anything.

A week later and we learn Joshua isn't HIV positive but has sciatica. When we arrive at the clinic, we wait fifteen minutes and the nurse calls us in. I know, almost for certain, it isn't awful news because she is smiling. Bad news travels fast—even the receptionist probably would have tipped us off. But their faces are sunny. We walk out of the clinic with a spring in our step but Joshua turns and says, "I know I've used up my chances."

Last night I watched a TV program about the tragic crash of golf pro, Payne Stewart's jet. Hearing the chase pilot's account, I see parallels in what we have experienced. The pilot spoke of feeling, "Very disheartened seeing Payne's Lear jet within fifty feet with frosted windows, knowing the passengers were unconscious, facing certain death and being utterly powerless to help in any way."

So similar to this disease, parents watch their children fly toward destruction and are helpless to intercede. Not frosted windows, but glazed eyes that cannot see, ears that cannot hear, messages sent but not received—just as if they are up 20,000 feet in a frozen depressurized cabin, asleep in the cockpit, flying out of control with an army of chase planes off to their right, rear, left and above; and no one and nothing but God can make the slightest difference.

Watching is worse than waiting. Highlighting every signpost, the experience lays out the full trip ticket and evolution from healthy child and family to full-blown addict and co-dependent enablers. The last thing is the macerated pulp of a life gone to hell. But move on, says the healthier part of my brain. Joshua sounds excited about school and wants to up his classes. Says a new girl he's met is motivating and inspiring him. She's almost graduated from college. My heart leaps but I reel it back—can't allow myself to be swept up and away. The disease is a master at creating pleasing fiction.

Can you believe it? This is the same kid who has quit or has been fired from a dozen jobs and now he's made employee of the month. Good golly—how in the world could he have come this far? God only knows and God gets full credit. As Joshua accepts the award, the nicest accolade his boss pays says more than the manager can ever know. "Joshua gives 100% even when he's sick" (referring to a cold, flu, etc.—not addiction, as he is unaware). Showing up day after day, Joshua works with this ongoing disease that mocks every effort.

Yes, Joshua does give 100% in spite of being sick, very sick. What was incomprehensible a year ago is now commonplace; life is improving and hope not a pipe dream. In two months he can drive again and in fourteen months he'll be off probation. How I pray it comes to pass; not just for Joshua but also for you. Right here, right now, is where we're all supposed to be. Joshua could never have come this far without the setbacks and I could never have learned the lessons I needed to practice without these trials and errors.

As Joshua moves forward, success strengthens and also threatens his recovery. He knows this and it frightens him. He will fly to Wisconsin in two weeks to visit a girl he barely knows on a university campus where every possible temptation will await him. He will be challenged and tested. Surrendering fear honors him and frees us both. Rather than strong-arm Joshua, I can offer a hand but not a handout. The outcome is unknown, but hope's kicked in and pushed dread aside.

*   *   *

Joshua returns today from his four-day impromptu adventure to Wisconsin, the visit with the girl he had known for less than forty-eight hours. I'm anxious to hear about it and relieved at this point, police, emergency room or hostess hasn't called with bad news.

112

Joshua's saga reminds me of the Bible parable, *The Prodigal Son.* A young, foolish boy brings shame and disgrace on his family. But the father, although sick at heart, lets his son go because poor choices will result in consequences leading the boy back to God and the family. And when that wonderful day arrives, the father runs—yes, runs (a most amazing thing for a dignified Jewish man of his era) to his beloved son and welcomes him home.

Joshua's trip to Wisconsin is uneventful. Relating the story, he sounds sorry he wasted time and money. I'm just relieved he seems okay. Thank God the enemy's in retreat. We don't have to climb Everest in a white out.

Then it happens again. Joshua doesn't answer the phone and I'm immediately shaken. Is this it? He's gone off the hook? What will fly at us this time? No, he only had his ringer off because he retired early and was exhausted. I'm still good and sick. Does one ever recover?

*   *   *

My dentist's office is in a rural setting next to a pasture of American bison. Since it rains frequently in the northwest, I barely paid attention when it showered, but noticed the large animals rose to their feet and grazed when it poured. Earlier, during a lull, the creatures slept and rested. But when the clouds broke, the great beasts were quick with the business of feeding.

I need to remember to rest and recuperate when there's a reprieve from this disease instead of worrying about something that's out of my control. And when the dark clouds drop their torrents, busy myself with distractions that feed and nourish me until the storm passes.

*   *   *

Bob's childhood friend, Larry, will never walk again. Hit head-on in a car accident, he is paralyzed from the chest down, presently in a trauma intensive care unit. Seeing this gentle soul supine on a rotating table—arms outstretched as if

113

nailed to a cross, bolts drilled into his skull, permanently, profoundly and forever humbles. Young and old victims on the unit, many on ventilators, eyes stunned and blank—all must be asking the same questions: Why me? What now?

A rehabilitation center for catastrophic injuries raises the bar of suffering. Addiction seems preferable to anything seen and experienced there. The horrific and ghastly head, spinal and burn injuries shock and shame me. These broken souls will never regain their former lives, but addicts learn their malady is treatable, and there is not only hope, but the promised return of previous social, spiritual and oftentimes physical function with a designed and proven program of recovery. However, those crippled by fire, head and spinal traumas are relegated to a permanence with no alternative. Wouldn't every one of them love a guarantee the scars would vanish, the cognitions return and the nerves regenerate?

Pain, all pain corners each of us. No one is spared, but what we do with struggles is our testimony. The strength of our character is never really tested until the bottom falls out. I have failed miserably at my exams, but I do believe I'm starting to learn.

Bob's friend is a delight saying please and thank you, instead of cursing and spitting at the world. He's thrilled with the tiniest improvements; a twitch of a shoulder, a pin's prick now perceived. He is resolute he will make the best of it. As I am learning, I shall make the best of Joshua's predicament. I will not wallow in self-pity but thank God I can *feel* the pain. Because feeling means life and life means hope.

*   *   *

Nearly a year has passed since Joshua got out of his third and hopefully last rehab. In that span of time we have accomplished much. He's been working, paying his bills, living on his own, almost finished counseling, probation and has completed two college courses successfully with an 'A' and a 'B'. He's almost earned his license back and is emancipating in a healthy fashion. We too, are taking better care of ourselves, not dropping everything to rush to his aid.

With signs of improvement, I've been easing back on my search to stabilize and divert attention. If I can make a meeting I do but if it's inconvenient I don't. Life feels good. Health is wealth or is naiveté is a cruel tutor?

But trust continues to erupt. We need to pick up things at Joshua's so arrange to get his apartment key from him at work. The message on the phone goes something like this: "Ah, gee, that sounds good, but when my girlfriend let herself into the building the manager jumped all over her. We're not supposed to let anyone use our keys and get into the complex."

Now that may be so but we doubt a manager would stop parents. Way back when I suggested we get an extra key for such occasions, he balked. He doesn't give us credit we'd never abuse that privilege. I suppose he wants his privacy or is it the addict's signature: Artful sleight of hand?

* * *

Joshua's sciatica is bearing down and taking me with him. He calls nearly every day. I hear the despair settle on his young shoulders; just when things are right, another sinkhole sucking him under. School's good, work's good. He gets his license tomorrow, but now this chronic, physical pain. Three months he's suffered. He has another doctor's appointment and I pray this time he will give Joshua a referral to a specialist, not prescribe something for the symptoms. I stay in the lobby while Joshua advocates for himself. Letting go, even in the little things is important.

The next day he gets his license back and it goes off without a hitch. It's hard to say what's more satisfying, the actual re-instatement of a privilege, or the fact that everything, absolutely everything falls into place. Rarely do things go this well. The disease teaches us never to expect it. The only cloud in this exquisite blue sky is his radiating back and leg pain. But in spite of it, his heart and mine are as light as swallows.

Spoke too soon—the phone just rang and it's Joshua. The car broke down but it doesn't surprise me. This is a rock in the road, not a plunge off a cliff. The old Karla would bark frantic orders, pace, fix and plot a rescue. Now I sit back and wait. This honors him and relaxes me.

*　　*　　*

Blisters and blessings: Painted reminders on cars and faces, graduations, a time of year crowded with memories and slivers of sorrow. Simple Pleasures: An honest day's work, a hot shower and a good magazine, a conversation with God and a healing heart. But Joshua's on my mind. It's summer, nice weather, he's almost twenty-one and talking about concerts and everything norms do. But he's not a norm, no matter how hard he pretends. He's come so far and has so much to lose. Will I ever stop obsessing?

*　　*　　*

Front-page news in the local paper: Homegrown scholar, athlete, all-round nice guy and super-star — drowned. Eighteen and about to go to college, deserved the best, and now this untimely loss of life, hope and promise. Many came to remember, eulogize and mourn this fine young man, Travis Olesen. I did not know him but I dreamed his dreams for my son. Now his dreams have ended and his parents are living a woeful nightmare. How unfair this popular and accomplished boy has been extinguished so soon; he did everything right and yet it turned out wrong.

Oh, dear parents—your pain is unimaginable. I pray my son will be worthy of the chance he's been given in spite of disease and wanton recklessness, a disease that freezes life in its young hour. If my son had died the many times he brushed death, few would have mourned him. Many would have bid good riddance and society might have felt relieved. I doubt if it can possibly lessen your pain but knowing your

116

son, a beloved and respected individual, left the world better, not worse, might be some measure of comfort.

I can only hope as Joshua recovers, he can someday be so loved and admired, that he can emulate Travis. That he can somehow give back to this great and hurting world. Somehow honor Travis and the countless others who have gone on prematurely and justify his existence with integrity and noble purpose. In so doing, perhaps his life can be redeemed and stand in tribute to those who went before him, or if not, as someone once said, "At least be a horrible warning."

* * *

Addiction gropes and violates like illicit hands invading private spaces. It can't be washed or wished away and forever robs, replays and taints. Like recovery from major surgery, first you lie still and sleep through the worst, then awaken and go in and out of the pain. Throat parched, lips cracked, you take a few sips and wait for it to get better. But better isn't easier. Like that first solo walk down the corridor, you stop and lean against the wall, catch your breath and hope you make it back alive.

How do I release what's buried in this mud flat? Life must wriggle free. Unsure, I take a tentative step and join an organization and attend a summer picnic with Bob at a beach house of one of the members. Walking in the door and facing dozens of strangers, we both are surprised by our confidence. Moving easily, meeting, greeting, glad-handing, it all comes back until I strut over to place my Chinese chicken salad on the table and trip and fall flat, sprawled in front of everyone with the bowl and contents jettisoned in a torpedo arc.

Although bruised, it seems inconsequential. People trip, people fall. It happens—it means nothing. That fall is a break-through.

Two social outings this week and the old Karla reappears; more relaxed, confident, more me. Not fully back, but the flat line's held in check. Little scary brushes with new people talking about their kids, fearing someone knows someone who knows Joshua, but fortunately that doesn't happen.

How can I ever go public with this? I want the book to help, but do I dare reveal this ugliness to open inspection? This isn't a travelogue or a cookbook. This is our life—the personal, private crawl through raw sewage. Do I want to stand exposed, pocked and pitted? How will I tolerate their eyes, those judging eyes? Yet, I feel *compelled* to write and reach out.

* * *

Joshua calls with good news. He got an 'A' on his psychology test. I gush but edit my exuberance. This disease conditions one to weigh all decisions, great and small. If I voice too much enthusiasm that might send a message my love is conditional. I'm still uncertain about many things. I'm sorry I set the bar so high and expected achievements that were my dreams, not his. But I mustn't buy into cause and effect. I cannot cause Joshua to succeed or fail in school, recovery or life. I'm not that powerful. No one is.

Time skips by stopping for nothing except the sweetness of surrender. Recovery comes with surrender, surrender to a Higher Power. The greatest troubles punctured life when pride and despair separated me from that Higher Power. But Al-Anon's become my Sherpa, leading me across crevasses that gobble bodies and minds. I'm not saying church isn't important, but Al-Anon is an intensive care unit that works in conjunction with the God of one's understanding.

Joshua has a Higher Power and I'm not it. It has to get really dark before you see the stars. Strangled by wishes infecting the bite, waiting is difficult medicine. But with rumpled, hollow heartaches, eventually you give up and go quietly.

Saturday afternoon the phone rings and Bob answers…a collect call from an out-of-county jail. Of course… it's Joshua. Just when we thought we were out of danger, it sneaks in the back door gripping the duct tape. We knew he hadn't been completely clean and sober, but thought mistakenly, he could drink in a controlled fashion. Obviously, he thought so, too. Why else would he risk everything when he had just put his life back together? He was arrested for underage drinking – an MIP (minor in possession) which breaks his probation. All this comes just *five* days before his twenty-first birthday. What he was so sure would never happen again (going back to jail) has happened, and the revolving door goes round and round.

For the first day I was numb. Second and third day very tearful and now I'm settling into acceptance. I go to meetings where I sob openly but feel supported. I call my sponsor and other Al-Anon friends, pray, shore Joshua up, but don't bail him out. We set boundaries and mourn our lot but don't shame him, for he is feeling bad enough. We grieve for Joshua, but also count our blessings. He was stopped before he drove drunk and killed someone.

Detachment eludes me. Rather, I've settled into flat nothingness. Not exactly indifference but resignation forced not elected. Not acceptance, not relief, but an acknow-ledgement of things as they are, have been and most likely will always be. I do not know peace but hope to capture it. Joshua has temporarily stepped up his resolve but it's only to placate us and fend the ogre in the dark. He will give in quickly to the call.

More hope erodes each time and along with it respect for him as he loses respect for the disease. He's cavalier in spite of looming consequences. It's amazing the ease at which he sweeps away the fear. I dread the possibilities but put that aside and focus on choices big and small.

Will we visit him in jail? Can we bring ourselves through steel doors that clang and bang? Muddy, brown and churning, his life is one thick lie. He lies to himself and everyone else. He juggled for a year, and a pretty good dance it was. But it was smoke and mirrors. He'll try again because the ride was a long one. He'll be more careful next time. He'll outsmart the monster, or so he'll tell himself. But sooner or later it comes back to bite. It takes another plug and runs into the dark.

Long ago, we expected Joshua to excel in school, sports and life. Then we settled for graduating high school, no more football. Then getting a GED and staying out of trouble; then getting a job. Now, it's our new expectation to see Joshua stay out of jail, not hurt anyone, contract AIDS or hepatitis. Not to have children he cannot parent, marry a woman he cannot commit to and go to college where he cannot finish. The disease adjusts expectations until only bare survival is the expected and realized outcome.

I'm mean, moody and prickly with trickle-down resentment. I feel razor contempt for Joshua's smugness. I want to smack that smirk off his face. I hate him, the self-serving addict who cares for nothing and no one but the rush. I hate hating him. I hate how it divides and conquers. I hate it all. I hate living with a disease that destroys from fifty miles away. I need a big cry. Why shouldn't I cry—a good, long, sobbing, retching, convulsive cry? A gut wrenching, fall to the floor, roll back and forth, sob screeching, arms slinging cry. Isn't it something to cry about? Yes, you dig through life but how many anticipate a buried landmine? It's unexpected but shouldn't be. Like the time I volunteered at an E.R. and someone handed me their severed thumb.

* * *

Broken dreams make me sad and mean. But after talking to Joshua, I remember there's another kind of parent pain, the pain of estrangement. Although Joshua's disease puts distance between us, through it all we know an undying commitment to one another. He calls this morning about business, but when hearing I'm sick with a cold suggests home remedies and says he loves me. That means so much. This son of mine is thoughtful and compassionate. When he isn't using, he is the kindest of human beings and even when he's toxic, he still loves me and I love him.

I am not worthy to judge Joshua and his recovery. I must remember I'm not his salvation and sometimes things must get worse before they can get better. None of my plans have worked out for my son. I have to admit my powerlessness over him. Also, I have to examine I've been searching for something outside of myself to heal and fill up the emptiness inside. There are no external solutions for internal problems.

This new self will no longer tolerate boring days and meaningless conversations. I will not call people I don't like or write people I don't care to hear from. I will not stay in contact with people whom I dread to see and will not feign interest where there isn't any. I will no longer pretend when I prefer authenticity. I will be cordial but never go out of my way for people who never return the same. I will tell it like it is if it is kind, necessary and true. I will stop inviting people first, calling more often and putting out greater effort. I will accept people as they are—self-absorbed and self-centered—and not take it as an affront or personal rejection. I will concentrate only on those who really love me, really matter and really care. I will not isolate but insulate from the takers and fakers and go on my serene and merry way—more alone, but less lonely. Authenticity is appealing, although setting aside people- pleasing is risky; the pay-off is self-respect.

Watching Oprah today, the topic is empty nest syndrome. Mothers complain as children leave for college. How I would love to be in that audience, "Just thank your lucky stars they're going off to *college*, not jail or rehab."

That distinctive long distance ring usually means Joshua. He must appear in court this Thursday because of the MIP and breaking probation. He's worried and I'm disgusted. I try to empathize until he says, "They're gonna steal everything from me." "Steal?" "You, you threw everything away. You don't work a program. You think you're some kind of special addict. You think you can get away with controlled use. God stopped you in your tracks. This disease will kill you. If I were the judge I'd put your butt in jail for a year, take your car away for three and maybe—just maybe— you'd start taking this seriously." Click—he hangs up. Now I'm even angrier. He screws up, I confront and he hangs up on me.

Well, I can wait this one out—he needs me more than I need him. I don't need this. I'm glad he's scared. I've been scared too—too many times to count. I'm glad he's sweating. I've walked the floor a million times. He will call me; I won't call him, and if he runs and fails to appear in court, oh well. If he falls off the earth, I will grieve. Oh, God, how I will grieve, but it will be over. How can one offer compassion when contempt poisons a heart?

* * *

Joshua goes to court today. When he hurts, I still hurt. My anger always gives way to empathy when I see despair in his eyes. He's scared but still not scared enough.

He's in a holding pattern and pleads not guilty to string it out and save money. He will keep his apartment if he goes to jail for three months or less and may sell his car in order to pay rent if necessary. He still ascribes this to bad luck, not poor choices. The disease convinces the host it's an innocent nuisance.

* * *

Crushing cravings are a cautionary tale. Clinical research suggests obesity is linked to a brain malfunction. The satiation signal in the obese is fourteen minutes

122

compared to ten minutes in average people. Those extra four minutes can add up to additional pounds. Although I'm normal weight, I have known and loved obese people and seen their hearts break as society shuns and holds them in contempt. Could it be the brains of addicts are different too? With a shift from addiction as a criminal matter to a health problem with bioclinical data to prove it, wouldn't that change everything?

With treatment and support, some recover. If more dollars were put into programs, rather than drug busts, prisons and border patrols, we might help more people. We're doing better but it's still not enough. When Joshua comes out of treatment he is motivated. But his rehab is always brief—a few short weeks. If he were able to stay, work and live for a year or two and then return to a world that does not label him bad but handicapped, it might improve his chances. Might—I'm not saying would. I don't have a lot of answers but I do have personal experience. Maybe none of this would assist the addict, but it could help families.

We are fighting a losing battle. The longest and most expensive war is the war on drugs. Prisons are America's growth industry. We will not stop the flood into this country. We tried prohibiting alcohol and that failed. Our dollars need to find the biological cause for addiction and treatment for the compulsion and cravings in the brain.

Ordinary people do not rely on chemicals; they do not need them regardless of hardship, but chemical dependents are driven to alter their minds. I believe this but I can't prove it. I only know my son owns his disease and does not blame it on us, his friends, his neighborhood, his childhood, society, pushers, dealers, music and media or anything but something deep inside of him.

Dear Lawmakers,   *September 28, 2000*

Thank you for your courage and tenacity to look at redirecting efforts related to drug offenses. Substance abuse is a terrible plague but with new legislation, a comprehensive and effective approach may win this war. Substance abuse is a disease and the problem isn't supply, but the deep-seated demand. Your vision for funds to be used for biological research and treatment is practical and compassionate. There are compelling statistics on the effectiveness of drug treatment. With a new approach and refocus, perhaps addiction can be conquered.

Sincerely, Karla V. Garrison

Like a stand-in playing second fiddle to a first love, I wait by the phone for Joshua's calls and work myself into frenzy. When he avoids us, it reinforces the fear this time is the BIG TIME, the time he's overdosed or is in so much trouble he's too ashamed to call.

He's out there now using more and more, but no new crisis he will admit to—just feeble attempts to explain himself. I have taught him how to treat me. I have accepted unacceptable behavior protesting with tears and verbal tirades. I must take control of what I can control. I can stop calling him. I can raise his empathy as he experiences our indifference. I can stop setting myself up.

Fact: I don't have to see or talk to him to survive.

Fact: I can choose how I want to be treated.

Fact: I can teach him what I will and will not accept.

Fact: I can tighten my boundaries.

What robust rhetoric. No longer shielded by savvy sense, brains are mush and musings of a fool. Of course, I cave in and leave a message that elicits a response. His excuses are disingenuous as I dissolve into tears. He apologizes in one breath and justifies his discourtesy in another. I must remember, if I can't control him, he can't control me, unless I give my power away.

Joshua called at 9:30 last night—very hyper, or was it crank? It was fifteen minutes of drivel. Says he's willing to sell his car to support his habit a while longer. His license and car were so important; now they've even taking a back seat to the disease.

Like a flag in a gale, he's a no-show—one and a half hours past due and doesn't return my call. I've been stood up and I'm fed up. It's amazing what you can get used to: Questions old as the hills, answers and alibis obvious and predictable.

He finally calls—no explanation but a weak apology. His boat's taking on water. I offer a raft, "Joshua, do you think you'd like to go back into treatment?" Quickly he replies, "No, no it's gonna be okay Mom." Not surprised by his answer, I sigh and tell him we love him, then say good-bye and go to bed. We're not going down with the ship.

The next week, I leave a message for Joshua. I make regular efforts to keep us from drifting apart. Although I often have the impulse to write him off, I remind myself how much he needs us—now, more than ever. Give them time to find themselves, even if it appears they've abandoned the search.

Joshua calls again moaning and groaning about impending consequences. I listen and work the program. I offer empathy, sympathy and a reality check. I avoid his pain. I think I did okay. I read for three hours without break-through worry. Best of all, his phone call came before 6:00 P.M., a boundary we set.

Before leaving to play at an open mic last night, I prayed my songs would be meaningful to someone. I should have also prayed for my memory to serve me. With rusty butterflies, I blew one song and forgot some lyrics. I faked it but was sure the audience squirmed with my embarrassment. Either that or they never caught on or perhaps thought I was suddenly struck and started speaking in tongues. I felt flushed, flustered, old and foolish; it shook my confidence out from under me. I used to have an excellent memory. I was a very quick study, memorizing pages and pages of dialogue in a script or hundreds of lyrics. Now I couldn't remember my *own* lyrics.

Has singing become my newfound penchant for suffering? Have I now replaced parent pain with public humiliation? Is that my penitence for unresolved guilt? The disease has me question everything. Whatever the reason, I have lost confidence to step on stage and sing. What was once as natural as breathing now leaves my palms clammy and heart racing.

Upon leaving the open mic, a middle-aged man stopped and shook our hands and asked if we were aware how much we had moved him, implying he had been a thorn in his parents' sides and now, as a parent himself, was able to look at it with new eyes. What I thought had been a waste of time, had in fact been meaningful to someone.

It's a quick jump to the next call when Joshua asks why I haven't inquired about his court appearance. I forgot and it wasn't on my mind. Whoa, I must be getting better—another slap on the wrist, no jail time, a fine and more after-care. That's it. Judge sees him as a mild risk with his solid work and school record. Theoretically, he can be free and clear in six months. He is hurting financially but that's good. He'll need to pick up more hours to pay his fines. All that worry. When will I ever learn? Just turn it over. Worry doesn't reduce tomorrow's sorrow; it weakens today's strength.

*   *   *

It is the last night of a seminar. I entertain the thought of introducing myself to a woman I find interesting but my mind quickly changes when she brags about her son, the football star, and even prefaces her monologue saying it isn't

126

bragging, just sharing. It turns off my interest in her and turns on my envy and heartache. But perhaps I'm getting healthier because I actually identify with the mother's pride and joy, since I once knew it. However, when she goes on and on, "We like to have him in sports because it keeps kids out of trouble," I can't sit by without speaking up. "Our son too, was a star athlete and honor student, until he became addicted...until he got sick, not in trouble, but came down with a disease that makes one powerless to stay *out* of trouble."

Yes, I'm still recovering from a life infected by this disease. From time to time I feel intense loss and pain. But I am no longer lost—no longer stuff feelings and accept what is unacceptable.

*   *   *

Joshua sings the blues and says he's hurting for money. He strikes a deal and Bob offers to let him stack wood for groceries. We set aside Sunday for him to come home, but of course he gets loaded the night before. We are complete idiots stuck on stupid.

Like a quantum shift with two parts in two places, one part of me is in a place of compassion, another in contempt. He can get to work, but to follow through with a commitment to us, one he set up, *he* wanted, forget it. Addicts promise but don't deliver. We have taught him how to treat us. It's time for a new lesson. Same behaviors get same results.

Joshua requests a couple of items from home, so we ask to drop them off as we're coming to Seattle for the weekend. After five calls we give up. It's obvious he's avoiding us. I've been upset for hours. I'd respect him more if he'd say, "Sorry Mom, I'm loaded, can't see or talk to you, love you, bye."

We haven't stepped foot in his apartment for months and the only contact now is when he calls or comes down to see us. We are only a convenience to an end. I'm not going to wait around today, waiting for that tomorrow that's really only today waiting in the future. Distant and cool, he's defensive and secretive. It's just days before Christmas, days before I tell my story at a big meeting. Will I be able to go through with it if all hell breaks loose?

If he overdoses, it's over. He'll be dead, really dead—not almost dead, not killing himself, but dead. I want to call, but must stand firm—say what I mean, mean what I say. Calling him sets me up for disappointment. Bob, obtuse and dismissive, says I shouldn't take it personally. I say, "Don't should all over me."

SIX

Circling the Wagons

2001

I'm the keynote speaker at a large AA/Al-Anon meeting where I tell my story:

Good evening. I'm Karla. I'm very happy to be here tonight. It's a privilege to have this opportunity to share among people who understand.

I've been in Al-Anon for three years and I am truly grateful for this program. When my sponsor urged me to consider speaking I was reluctant. One of my defects is perfectionism, so it was easy to convince myself the time wasn't right because I had not perfectly perfected the program. But now I'm aware it's progress, not perfection that's important.

I was born in San Antonio, Texas but grew up in California and have lived all over the world. I'm an only child. My dad was addicted to alcohol and chasing women, and my mom was addicted to Dad. After seventeen years in a violent, abusive marriage, they finally divorced. It was something I had always wanted.

The first time my dad hit my mother was in the middle of the night when I was nine years old. I awoke to her screams and ran to the living room where she sat on the sofa and my father stood before her and slapped her back and forth with his open hand until he broke her eardrum. I remember grabbing one of the heavy volumes from the set of encyclopedias neatly shelved on the wooden stand in the hallway, returning to the living room and whacking it hard against his back. But the blow, like the little girl I was at the time, had no effect except to send me running for help.

Neighbors called the police and I hid by a bush on the front lawn as my father was cuffed and placed in a squad car. That evening Mother left my dad again and we packed and moved to Texas. Now you might ask, why would any woman endure, much less expose her child to such maltreatment, especially an intelligent and educated woman.

The reasons are complicated with layers that confound and confuse. In my mother's case, she was widowed at twenty-three when her first husband was killed at Guadalcanal only forty-five days into the marriage, left after six weeks when her second husband announced he didn't really think he loved her after all and was also beaten and battered by a violent father who favored her younger sister.

Vivian was my mother, the oldest of two daughters and although plain, the kindest and sweetest. She was born to be a mother, born to hold a hand when you wake at night and first to listen or give in. Her laugh was infectious and warm smile drew strangers on a park bench who would give up secrets no one else had heard. She was funny and smart and earthy and real. She survived rheumatic fever and a year in bed when she was twelve and the rest of her days with swollen ankles and a life cut short by heart failure.

She was a first grade teacher of migrant children she loved and hugged and inspired. She told them they could go to college and some believed and returned years later to thank her for breaking the cycle of stoop labor. She put me on a pedestal and convinced me I could do anything, but she wasn't perfect. A realistic rendition demands the truth. She was afraid of death and dying and sickness and disease and passed those fears on to me. She had loose boundaries and told me things I didn't need to hear but she was my best friend and I would have gladly died for her with a smile on my face.

I learned early on my family was different. Mom was always leaving and reconciling with my father. Consequently, I changed schools sixteen times and never knew from day to day if we'd be packing and moving. Therefore, I learned quickly to build walls, burn bridges and keep secrets. I became an accomplished loner and never felt like I fit in. Because my dad was frequently quitting or losing jobs, our homes varied from modest to shabby shacks; some so bad I remember having people drop me off several blocks away so they would not know where we lived. One year was especially tough. Although Mom was a teacher, the heart disease interrupted her work. We were so poor that summer we ate nothing but tomato sandwiches for breakfast, lunch and dinner.

At an early age I made a conscious decision not only to get a good education but also never to marry an alcoholic. I would have a stable family, a beautiful home and I would bring dignity to my life. I became very determined to set goals and achieve them.

While in college, I met my husband and we were a perfect match. He too, was the hero of his alcoholic home, and we were determined to put that behind us. We would create a healthy family. We had careers, saved our money, and waited to have children. We'd do everything right: From Scouts to Sunday school and Little League, I would be a stay-at-home mom, preparing dinners we would enjoy every evening.

Life hummed along nicely until I was thirty and five months pregnant with Joshua, our second son. My mother was hospitalized in ICU with heart trouble, and two days later my appendix ruptured. I had eighteen inches of bowel removed and was also in another ICU.

This was the first test that shook our little world. Then, six months later, when Jason was a three-year-old and Joshua a newborn, my mother threw a pulmonary embolism the day after I brought her home from the hospital following open-heart surgery. She never regained consciousness and died the next morning on Halloween. I nearly collapsed with grief. I had two precious sons, a wonderful husband, and a great life but my dear mother was gone. I felt like an orphan. At the time I couldn't imagine any worse pain. But little did I know it was only a preview of coming attractions.

As I slowly came back to life, things were good for the next dozen years or so. We had this great American family, my husband was in the Army and we got to travel all over the world. We had two wonderful boys, lots of friends and a beautiful home. Life was good until that inauspicious occasion when our sons became adolescents and the aliens kidnapped them. Only the invaders didn't come in UFO's, but bottles, pipes and pills. Both our sons began to drink and drug. With this, we were ushered into the darkest decade of our lives.

Our older son drank and smoked pot in high school, but he has gone on to be a good husband, father, son and provider, who doesn't drink, drug or smoke. Our younger son, not only drank and did pot, but went on to become a full-blown meth addict. The poison transformed him from a gentle soul into a hideous monster, violent, volatile and absolutely insane. It got so bad I barely escaped with my life.

Paralyzed with grief, I isolated and pushed people away. I envied healthy families and was clinically depressed for years. I just couldn't believe this was happening to our son, a happy, well-adjusted honor student and star athlete. This was supposed to happen to kids from broken homes, kids who were hurting and troubled—kids like my husband and I were. And we never used illicit drugs. I was dumbfounded but rolled up my sleeves and searched for answers. Was it because I had major surgery when I was pregnant and was heavily sedated for a week? Was it because I was a walking zombie his first year as I grieved my mother's death? Why couldn't I fix this? I had always set goals and achieved them, but now I felt like a failure.

You see, I didn't understand the disease. I didn't realize Joshua was a sitting duck in this genetic soup. Like his grandfathers on both sides, he was waiting to answer the call. Fortunately, we got into treatment and found our way to Al-Anon. Today we're not perfect and our younger son isn't clean and sober but we're making progress and still love one another.

What brought me this far is amazing grace, family, this program, sponsor, friends and writing, too. I started a journal that evolved into a manuscript I hope to have published. And I also composed songs. I would wake in the middle of the night and hear music and lyrics in my head. I felt compelled to record them into a little cassette and then begged my husband to accompany me on his guitar. In the remaining time, I'd like to finish telling my story by sharing three of these songs.

The speaker's meeting is a success. I remember the lyrics and come away confident and encouraged. But addiction continues to prove itself an endurance contest. When the disease kicks in we are the first who get blown off, put off, dodged and dissed. We rarely hear from Joshua. He's dropped out of college, is going to quit his job and move in with friends we've never met. They live in a town an additional half-hour away, making his drive for counseling longer. My peace and serenity are shaky. I have to remember happiness is not circumstance-dependent but a direct result of self-talk.

* * *

I arrive late at Al-Anon but I'm the first to be handed literature to read. The topic is grief about a son who jumps from a bridge to his death. That was Joshua's first ideation and the words stumble from my throat.

133

Two women in the meeting have lost children to suicide. Another woman says her daughter is clean and sober but they rarely see or hear from her. I hug the mother who is drenched in sadness at the recent suicide of her addicted son. I remind myself to count my blessings. When Joshua drops by we exchange affection. I must remember parents who have neither expressions of love nor the physical presence of their children.

But in spite of good intentions, the disease tests me time and again. The latest began with a late night call from Joshua. "I'm sick, really sick. I saw a doctor and its bronchitis. I need to come to your place and rest, but that's one long drive."

"So what are you going to do?"

"Well, I guess I'm gonna have to drive my ass down there, aren't I? But I'M SICK!"

Once again, remaining composed, "You're welcome to come and recuperate. I'll leave the key; let yourself in and I'll put the vaporizer on. Wake me if you need to. I love you. Drive carefully. "

The next fourteen hours Joshua sleeps and lets his body rest. Here he is at twenty-one, fighting bronchitis, and eight years ago I grounded and first spanked him in this very room when I found him experimenting with tobacco. With his upper respiratory history of chronic colds and croup, I knew smoking would be especially hazardous. I warned, admonished and lectured and still, *still* he experimented and became addicted. I want to slap the shit out of him, not hold his hand. He abuses his body and his body rebels. The next twenty-four hours we do this dance; my anger flares, his counters. I feel guilt and apologize; he concedes he's ruining his health.

Saturday, Bob and I had our first appointment to see a recording studio. The meeting went okay but clearly there is a generation gap. The guy is about twenty-six and it's obvious he thinks we're ancient. I have to respect him though; he didn't schmooze us trying to close the deal but I left feeling old and foolish.

Upon returning home, we find Joshua in a sentimental mood. After a pleasant evening we say our goodnights and go to bed. About a half-hour later as we're dropping off to sleep, he pokes his head into our room and whispers, "Dad, Mom, I want you to know how much I appreciate all you've done for me and I really do love you. Good night."
"Good night honey, we love you, too."

Another hour passes and again he opens our door. "Mom, can I talk to you?" "Yeah," I say fresh in the fog. "No, I mean can you come downstairs so we can talk?" *Oh no. What now?* His voice blows the sleep from my mind. I know that tone; know what *that* means, incoming rockets.

Part of recovery is disarming the power of secrets. Joshua, like all chemical dependents, carries hefty sorrows and a clutch of sins that haunt him. Unloading burdens not only displaces pain but also empowers him. Honest confessions are essential but excruciating for a parent. I shouldn't be his sponsor, yet I am frequently drafted.

I slink down stairs and my mind races—what bomb this time? What life-altering juncture? Joshua opens the floodgate and the torrent rushes forth. He's been using heavily—also meth. He was fired three weeks ago. He's depressed and scared but still not ready to recover. He's a walking skeleton, coughing blood, broke, unemployed and desperate. He's about to lose his apartment but *still* not ready to go to treatment. I can only listen and let him purge...I am powerless to do anything else.

He explains he didn't come to me earlier because I was cold and distant. I didn't want to hear bad news. I have now re-thought that, among other things. My serenity is my responsibility, not his, and a loving family depends on each other as sounding boards. As long as I don't enable, I am not hurting him or me.

I suggest meetings and in-patient but he replies, "Mom, you know how that young guy at the studio couldn't relate to you and vice versa? Well, that's how it is at meetings. The majority of those people are generations older than me. Can you understand?" I admit he has a point.

He cries and ventilates and I pat his back and feel tremendous sympathy for all of us and all of you. Many addicts don't "get it" until they've returned to rehab several times and are in their forties—that's more than twenty years for him. Our time is running out. Is yours?

I grieve for Joshua, not that it came as a surprise, but because it didn't. First I am numb and supportive and then sink into despair; now on the fifth day, I'm counting my meager blessings. He was fired because he was sleeping one off, not because of moral turpitude. He was fired because of his disease. It's easy to imagine gratitude will adjust as time goes on, as time has been.

It may one day look like this:

He's in prison but not for a violent crime.
He's alive and not insane.
He's in prison but not for life.
He's in the mental hospital but not in prison.
He's on the street but not in the mental hospital or prison.
He's still alive and we hear from him occasionally.
He doesn't have HIV and is still alive.
He has hepatitis but doesn't have HIV.
He has HIV but not full-blown AIDS.
He's recovering from pneumonia and is off the ventilator.
He still has teeth and hasn't developed emphysema.
He has emphysema but not lung cancer.
He has lung cancer but it's in remission.
He has liver disease but he's a candidate for a transplant.
He never graduated high school but he has his GED.
He didn't finish college but has a B+ average.

He doesn't have a career but he has a job.
He doesn't have a job but he doesn't steal or deal.
He has a phone as long as he pays the bill.
He doesn't own a home but he has an apartment.
He doesn't have an apartment but he has a room.
He doesn't have a room but he's not under a bridge.
He needs a haircut but not a bath.
He needs a bath but not a clinic to treat his open sores.
He has a car but no money for gas.
He doesn't have a car so he doesn't need gas.
He's painfully thin but doesn't have to diet.
He can still walk, talk, see, hear, think, hug and visit.

Having him alive is the consolation prize. Like any type A carcinogen, the monster metastasizes and invades the healthy and renders them morbidly useless.

Days pass and Joshua answers our call and leaves a message on the machine. This is the only way we communicate. If we call at a time when he's sleeping or loaded, he won't pick up. We must wait to hear from him, and that's not altogether bad. I leave upbeat messages and hope he returns the calls.

When I hear that familiar long distance ring, I get both excited and anxious. The phone still holds me hostage. He reports he's "okay," but experience tells me otherwise. If he had found a job, he would call; if he hasn't, it's because he's partying until the last minute—or, worst of worst, he's hustling and money is no longer an issue. The task is acceptance. A meeting, a few days of stinging sadness, a gut-wrenching cry or two and I'm back among the living.

Since we have to be in Seattle today, I call Joshua to see if we can meet and have dinner with him, but the conversation shrivels in response to a couple of questions: Has he found out what he's going to do, and where does he want his life to go?

After vague responses, it's clear he still isn't working or pursuing employment. Agitated and emphatic, he insists he isn't stealing but rage bubbles and we argue. He ends the call saying he doesn't think he can meet us because he has so much to do. I shoot a nasty retort and we hang up.

Within a couple of minutes, I call back crying and demanding him to answer. Another ten minutes pass and I dial a third time. "Joshua, I know you're ignoring me. I want to be really clear. If you don't answer, I will not be available the next time you get sick and need a shoulder to lean on." Not a minute later the phone rings.

I pick up, fur fluffed and claws out. "It's a damn good thing you called back!" I scream. "I've had it with you dictating the parameters of this relationship! You will not determine when and how we will see you! We are your parents and we WILL see you today at five o'clock and we WILL have a nice dinner and ENJOY it!" He quickly replies, "You're crazy you know—really crazy—you're just as crazy as someone using."

He's right but I say nothing. His opinion of me is none of my business. "Be there at 5:00 P.M.!" Click.

I'm restless and confused. When I'm supportive and compassionate, am I also condoning irresponsibility? But if I express contempt, does it serve a good purpose? *Nothing* motivates him. You can't reason them back to where they need to be.

Is addiction nature's way to weed and cull? Is natural selection politically correct? There is for example, the tale of a drunken man killed by a tiger when he entered its enclosure in a Calcutta zoo and tried to hang flowers around its neck. Did he accidentally improve the gene pool by removing himself from it?

Surprisingly, Joshua comes down for the weekend to avoid temptation and strengthen his resolve to start anew—

his choice, not at our insistence. We attend church together, sit for an hour and hear a sermon titled, "Building a Better Parent." The young, talented pastor, who grew up in an alcoholic home, begins to preach and teach. It's obvious he has residual resentments toward his alcoholic parents, and his message, like everyone's, is shaped by personal experience. He describes four principles of great parenting:

1. **GREAT PARENTS TEACH IN NONCONFLICT SITUATIONS**. They take every opportunity to explain, model and reinforce values during peaceful, happy times.

2. **GREAT PARENTS TEACH THE MORAL REASON WHY**. Great parents explain the moral and ethical reason behind principles and lessons, boundaries and limits.

3. **GREAT PARENTS CREATE AN ATMOSPHERE OF JOY**. They build a home that is safe, loving, nurturing and fun.

4. **GREAT PARENTS WORK HARD TO BUILD TRUST AND HONOR**. Children with strong foundations, have tools to resist stealing, pre-marital sex and drugs.

At this point Bob gets up and leaves the service. Ironically, I feel no anger because we applied these principles. Even Joshua pats my hand and says, "Mom, you and Dad are great parents. Nothing I do is your fault."

The young pastor doesn't understand. My heart goes out to him. If he should be so unfortunate his children, who are still young, acquired their paternal grandparents' genes for addiction, how then will he preach? Will he compose sermons that edify and comfort or blame and shame?

Oh yes, I'm not a perfect parent and certainly not a great Christian. I sin, curse, covet and judge, but who is perfect? And what parent is? I'm working on being better,

139

but that's beside the point. This is a disease, not the result of poor parenting.

As the minister proceeded to admonish, I felt God telling me I had done a good job and had not caused this affliction. While Joshua sat there and consoled me, I wanted him to jump up and defend us to the pastor, to the world. But real peace is quiet assurance.

Upon leaving the service a woman sitting next to us turned and said, "This must be your son; he sure is a nice young man." I replied, "You think so? Yes, he is."

I wanted to add but didn't, "Yes, he is—a wonderful young man—and also a meth addict." We never stepped foot in that church again.

Brazen bulletins won't stop this epidemic because it's not about saying no or bashing parents. It's about a genetic code. From the beginning, these people are born different. Just ask any of them. One can preach and teach, but they're going to do what they are programmed to do.

Joshua is poisoned by this plague and experiencing a crisis of belief. I can't blame him as I have questioned my own faith. Over and over and over again we have all prayed for his healing. I still believe God can perform this, is more than capable of doing so, but for some reason unwilling, at least at this time. Joshua believes God has better things to do than help him. He feels hopeless. I too, have sat next to that enemy and felt the shackles chain me to despair. How, oh how, he longs to be normal, to enjoy life—plain, beautiful, mundane life—without the call, without the pull into the darkness.

He reports all efforts to obtain a good job are fruitless because applications now ask about arrests and convictions. He says he'd rather be a bum than go back to flipping burgers. He may get his wish. Faith floats away on an undercurrent of certain uncertainty.

Like vampire finches of the Galapagos, the disease

drains energy and vigor. Joshua's supposed to be here, spend the night and attend make-up after-care counseling in the morning. That faraway feeling tells me to expect him to be a no-show. Sure enough my hunch is right. I pull into the drive and his car isn't there. I draw a deep breath and dial his number but do not expect to find him in such bad shape. "Mom, I just can't drink. Last night, honest to God, I had no intention to do meth but I'm absolutely powerless. I want you to know I love you. That's why I answered your call but I can't talk right now. I'm telling them Monday what's up and even if I have to go to jail, I need in-patient—but please, please, this isn't a good time to talk. I'm okay; I'm not going to kill myself, I just need to go."

"Joshua, it's gotten bad, hasn't it?

"MOM! I need to come off this and don't want to talk right now. I answered you because I knew you'd be worried."

"Yes Joshua, I'm very worried. Please don't shut me out; please open up."

"Mom, I love you—I'm gonna get help—I'm sorry— don't worry." Click.

Don't worry? Don't worry! Don't die on me!

Is love answering the phone when you're loaded? My head's locked in a cage with a rat smacking its lips.

*　*　*

Today is Bob's fiftieth birthday and the disease has its way. After two days of calling Joshua to remind him, the anxiety mounts. As every hour passes we click through the probabilities: Death from overdose, jail, suicide, shame too thick to penetrate, news too awful to bear. Knowing full well he is spiraling fast, it's always at the back of our minds, chewing and crippling us.

Quite unexpectedly the phone rings and its Joshua. He awakes mysteriously from a stupor, coming down, crashing off crank. He's been asleep for two days and God must have awakened him as his ringer is off. How this strengthens faith. Our sick son is alive but in grave condition. But this reminds us, if God has power over sleep, God has power over anything.

Dear Beloved Son,   *March 25, 2001*
I miss you tonight. I miss your voice, hug and presence. I would call you now but you would not be there. And if you were, you still would not. Your body would answer, your voice speak words but you are far away and only the shell of you remains——your demented twin.

While at sea we must be content with your stand-in. I will pray for you while you drift, while you sail on currents swift and perilous and await your safe return.

Oh what a day, when you put down permanent anchor in that peaceful harbor—safe, restored in mind, body and soul.

I will wait and never stop waiting. I will look toward that horizon as you appear in the light of a new tomorrow. Let my love be your compass home.

Forever, Mom

I just called Joshua and left a message knowing full well he would be asleep or worse. In so doing I could avoid disrupting my serenity. "Hi Honey, it's Mom. Just wanted to give you a call and say I was thinking of you. Hope you're okay; we're all fine here. Going to take Holly to the groomer. Your family loves you and if you need to talk, we're here for you. Hope to hear from you. Love you, bye." He's staring down the barrel of his pipe dream. Until he realizes his wanting cannot cross over into doing, he will continue to self-implode.

Usually, I can expect to hear from Joshua every week. He didn't disappoint. It was seven days and he called; so relieved to hear his message and not the least bit surprised by his complaints. Meth transposes the brain with each use making everything less, not more. Great and simple pleasures are reduced to the monotonous; Disney World becomes a shuffle down a gravel drive to the mailbox.

* * *

Making the bend to Joshua's rental house at Alki Beach, I hardly comprehend the possibilities at first. I see two rescue vehicles speed past and is that a helicopter hovering just ahead? Now the traffic stops and lots of lights and commotion fringe of our vision. "Should we park here and walk?" I ask Bob. Always reluctant to wait, this seems logical, so he pulls over and we get out.

"How far is it?" I inquire.

"Just ahead," he answers, as we move up the sidewalk where groups of people cluster. I hear something about police, but don't get the details. Another dozen steps and I stop cold and grab Bob's arm.

"Oh God, what if it's Joshua? What if there's been a drug bust?" my voice, now an octave higher, as I wobble with worry.

"Do you want to go back?" Bob tosses.

"I don't know, I don't know, let's give him a call." With no answer my mind leafs through the original assumption. Can I do this? Should we do this? "How much farther is his house?"

"Just a bit," Bob says, as we clutch each other and snake our way through crowds of people and caution tape.

There it is—a police car totaled and six or seven cars involved—just this side of Joshua's house. Relief sweeps over me although paranoia is perfectly in place. If we had turned back, we would have missed a pleasant visit with him. But if I had been correct, could I ever have erased the sight of Joshua handcuffed in a squad car or face down on the front lawn? Since he was absent for Bob's birthday and Easter, I'm even more thankful we carved this pleasant memory, since they are so few and far between. Happiness is no longer a natural process, but a conscious, measured choice.

Weeks pass and resentment builds. I figure it's time to talk it out, not act it out. I call not expecting him to answer but he does. "What's up?" he asks with raspy hoarseness.

"Joshua, I need to talk."

"Ohhhhh…kay…" he answers.

"I've been really missing you and feel frustrated that we never get to see you."

"You know why, Mom. I really don't want to talk about this. You know what's up. You know I don't want to hurt you, but I don't want to see the judgment in your eyes."

"What you would see is joy not judgment. We want to see you. What's so awful about that?" I'm crying now but not raising my voice. "We know you're on a binge, we aren't going to lecture, we just want to see you."

"I'm sorry Mom, I'm really sorry. You know I love you guys. I'll always love you but I can't stop and it takes over and comes first," he explains. "I'll see you tomorrow." I interrupt, "Please Joshua, don't make promises—it gets my hopes up too much. Just try to call more often."

"Mom, I'm sorry, I really do love you. Someday it'll be better."

We part with love you's and so it goes, life loving an addict.

The following week he tells us he loves us again. He sounds okay and says he's going to call more often. We make small talk and try to keep it pleasant. The call lasts a minute but I treasure whatever I can get. It's hard to know what to talk about. It's not like, "Well, what have you been up to?" We know what he's been up to. It's not like we can say, "How's work and school?" because there is no job, no longer school. What does a parent talk about to an addict?

"So Joshua, how are you and your room-mate dividing chores?"

"Oh, we're mass cool; he's just as neat and organized

144

as I am so it's cool, real cool."

"So how's your sciatica?"

"It's better now that I'm not lifting," referring to his job as a bellman.

"Well, that's good honey—really good. It's really good to hear from you, too, we love you and love hearing from you."

"I love you guys, too. Well, I'm gonna go now, okay?"

"Call us any time."

"Okay, yeah, peace, love you."

"Love you too, love you always."

Addiction is bracketed with guilt and compulsion. Guilt in the nonaddicted constrains, guilt in the addicted cripples. Guilt in the nonaddicted cordons off self-recriminations; guilt in the addict takes over and takes charge. Addicts do nothing in moderation, including penance. Unconscious guilt may extract an even higher price.

Freud observed that some people (might we include addicts, too?) resist therapies designed to extinguish guilt. Does the addict, does Joshua, cling to suffering because in punishment of self, he seeks atonement for crimes both conscious and unconscious? Guilt may to some degree control the masses but not without cost. Some guilt is appropriate and even necessary, but most guilt is an exaggerated response to infractions.

A friend recently confessed guilt about a comment she made regarding her husband. While doing lunch and making small talk, she told me she had wished him dead while he was active in his disease. I thought nothing of it, nodding who wouldn't wish that? When one sits at the bedside of terminally ill loved ones, who doesn't want the suffering to end?

What I soon forgot ate at her for days and compelled her confession. But her healthy guilt spawned remorse, not self-hate. All of us from time to time engage in acts we know or feel to be morally wrong. Our difference from addicts is we recognize we have made mistakes but do not cross over to that place where we believe we *are* mistakes.

Once ensnared, time and again addicts betray their ethics. With each transgression they move farther away from the nonaddicted, the morally pure as they see us. That's when the guilt and "F—its" increase. Do addicts douse original pain? Or do addicts do what they do, suffer pain and douse the consequences of what they do?

It's that familiar long distance ring. Since its Tuesday, not Wednesday, I figure it's too soon to be Joshua. Most meth addicts have three-day highs followed by three-day crashes. It's unrealistic to think he's awakened this soon after a binge weekend. But, by golly it is my son calling to chat rather than ask for a favor, moan or groan. I purposely focus on the moment of having him alive and talk about happy things and skip over the rest.

"Mom?"

"Hi, Hon—how you doing?"

"I'm doin' okay, I guess. How are you and Dad?"

"We're okay, but we've had colds."

"How long has it been since I've seen you?" he asks.

"It's been nearly a month—a long time."

"Wow, you want to have lunch or something tomorrow?"

"Of course, anything, anytime."

"Can you like drive halfway or something?"

"Since I have so far to go to work, I'd really like it if you could come down here. You could spend the night and break up the drive."

"Okay…but if I need to roll, I'll have to take off."

"I understand."

"I know you're worried but I'm okay—just depressed. I want you to know I'm a leader among friends. I

146

haven't stolen anything. I try to talk them out of it, too. It's my business if I want to put something in my body."

"Well, we'll look forward to seeing you tomorrow. I love you and I'm glad you called."

"Love you too."

* * *

When he says he's coming and actually shows up, it's more than a treat—it's a miracle. His smile warms me from a block away and his desperate hugs melt my heart. Miracle too, is the joy I feel without a hint of malice. My beloved son is home for a visit. Every mother, every parent knows what I mean.

While watching TV together, I come over to the big lounge chair where Joshua is sitting. Without needing to ask, I casually sit on his lap and curl in his arms...the sweet symbiosis of mother and child. While he cradles me, I whisper, "I'm so glad you're my son."

Answering with puzzled amazement, "You are?"

"Yes, I really am." With my response his body goes limp and he turns his head away, sobbing quietly, overcome with a mother's unconditional love. Bob looks up and asks without saying, what's wrong? What happened? And then with words unspoken, knows somehow what has just transpired.

"I'm sorry you're sad Joshua," I try to comfort. "I know you've been sad for so long."

As his pain surfaces, he tries to recover. "I don't want to feel this. How can you say you're glad I'm your son?"

"Because you *are* a wonderful boy."

Quickly, knowing the feelings are overwhelming, I scoot from his lap and move to the sofa so he can regain his dignity.

Joseph Merrick, the Elephant Man, thought he was a terrible disappointment to his mother, but no son as gentle and loving could ever be a disappointment.

Karla Klear Sky

SEVEN

Base Jumping

2001

For twelve years I've taught court- ordered domestic violence offenders how to talk it out, not act it out. I've had 250-pound soldiers threaten my life and later eat out of my hand. I emphasize violent behavior is learned and can be unlearned.

The past perpetrators march across my mind: Service members from every military branch referred to Fort Lewis; family members, men and women as young as eighteen and a couple in their eighties who regularly slapped each other around. There was the regal nurse married to a colonel who stabbed him in the thigh with a steak knife but minimized her abuse saying, "I wasn't aiming for the femoral artery." Then the young freckle-faced troop who put his wife's panties between bread and mustard and took a bite before her disbelieving eyes as he protested her purchase of lingerie instead of lunch meat; the staff sergeant who shot at his wife with a crossbow but missed; the black grandmother who pulled a hunk of hair out of a stranger's head in the Exchange checkout line; the German girl who cut up her husband's favorite shirt into one-inch pieces; the female corporal who tried to run her husband over with their pickup truck and the sixty-seven-year-old retired Navy petty officer whose older brother sexually molested him for years.

I remember the mother of two sets of twins who bashed in her husband's windshield with a baseball bat; the obsessive/compulsive who broke his girlfriend's rib when he found a pubic hair on a bar of soap; the petite, Puerto Rican beauty who would say, "Ohhhh, we gonna rumble," as she swung a hot curling iron whenever her husband came home late; the nineteen-year-old with a pregnant teenage wife saying, "Yeah, I kicked her in the stomach, but she wasn't even showin' yet." The guy who broke his son's third grade teacher's nose when he refused to change a report card; the blue-eyed blonde lieutenant who strangled and revived his wife three times on their honeymoon and the guy from Kansas who landed in the victim's group after his wife went berserk when she learned he'd been having a six-year affair with his mother.

I saw scores of offenders, most who never changed, but some adopted non violence. How gratifying and yet, I cannot break my son's destruction, cannot peek around corners and find the secret door that unlocks his heartache. Hollow and aching, we're trapped in a mirrored hall.

For all this time I've never said a word to staff, much less students, about the secret that crowds my heart. Oh, I've shared my father was an alcoholic and my husband's father too, but none of the people at work know how far the disease has reached into our primary family.

Yesterday, upon learning one of my students graduated from the same high school Joshua attended, I felt compelled to disclose. This nice, twenty- year-old recovering alcoholic, sober one year and two months relapsed and got into an altercation with his wife. According to the report it was a minor incident but left him feeling bad because he thought he had licked his alcohol problem.

After class I asked if he had hit bottom when he decided to get sober and what was his formula. He reiterated he wanted to stop living like that. Looking for an opening, I blurted, "Did you know my son, Joshua Garrison—he went to your high school?" "Yeah, he played football, right?" he asked. "Yes, he lettered in Varsity as a sophomore. You know he's an addict and has been to rehab three times. He's still not doing well, although for a while he was working and going to college." It spills but the soldier only says, "Oh," as his eyes dart for the exit.

It's clear I placed an unfair burden on this kid's shoulders. He didn't know what to do or say. It was suddenly quiet and I felt embarrassed for my unprofessionalism. I told him how much I admired his honesty and commitment to recovery, not only from alcoholism, but also from violent behaviors, then said goodbye and privately kicked my butt. Lives that intersect do not entitle us to cross boundaries for self-serving motives.

*   *   *

It's late May of 2001 and we find a recording studio and an engineer closer to our age. He's a seasoned professional. We also meet with the session players to rehearse for the CD, but I have horrible laryngitis. Never in my life have I had allergies but this spring I developed them. In spite of meds and rest, I can barely speak, much less sing. But sing I do and how right it feels. I'm never so alive, so in my element than when I perform or when singing or public speaking.

Since we don't know the musicians, I feel tense but that soon evaporates with the magic of the music. My songs, my lyrics, no—God's songs, God's lyrics—come to life and fill the studio with a pulse of energy and the glow of recovery. My voice is shot but my soul soars. It's coming to fruition—this journey, this mission of carrying the message.

Of course, suspended between hope and fear, the disease hits the fan again. Joshua and his roommate must leave the beach house. The landlord wants them out. They sat back pretending the day wouldn't come and come it has.

Our first hint things are falling apart is Joshua saying he is coming down to spend the night. Friday night? That can only mean something big and bad. What twenty-one year-old addict spends Friday night with parents?

151

He hits the house like a hurricane with wild, pressured speech. He makes landfall and we duck and cover as he roars through rooms processing the inevitable. With each thunderous step, his big, white tennis shoes announce the arrival. He curses the disease and unravels. Every place he looks for an apartment rejects his application. Even with a year's good rental history and the job at the hotel, things look bleak.

We explore options, rooms and kitchenette motels. "When doors slam shut, God's leading you in another direction," I offer.

"I don't even know if He cares about me. My life is shit. Josh Garrison's life is shit!"

"What would make you happy?"

"I'd like to get off this damn probation, have a part-time job and a small apartment and be able to use without getting arrested. I'd like this asshole landlord to stop screwing with me. I'd like everyone to know drugs are everywhere, *everywhere*, and there's no getting away from them and if people aren't hurting anyone they should leave us alone."

"Is that why the landlord's kicking you out?"

"Mom, I want you to know I haven't done anything bad except for drugs. I just want my life manageable."

"Joshua, you know what's making it unmanageable."

"Yeah, I know Mom—I'm not there yet."

The next morning finds him in better spirits but Bob and I blistered from the close encounter. He takes off early to make arrangements and we collapse most of the afternoon.

The following week ends with another call. Our attachment and estrangement wax and wane like wind and current; there's a rhythm that follows and leads, a little disappointment here, a game of tag there, an apology, a tear, a tearing down, a building up. The most recent fly-by shakes me with its concussion.

152

"Mom, I need to come down and get a few things from the attic; we got an apartment."

"Fine, we'll look forward to seeing you," I reply. "When are you coming?"

"Tomorrow; I need the stuff right away."

"Okay—well, I won't be home until mid-afternoon. Why don't you come by about 7:00 P.M. after the rush?"

"Naw, I want to come about 2:00 P.M. I'll let myself in with the key."

"Well...actually we've moved the key," I answer, waiting for the effect.

"Oh—that's good, the addict can't have the key now? I'm not gonna to steal from you guys! I don't steal from *anyone*!"

"If you'd let me explain...we don't think you would but someone with you might. We're just taking care of ourselves. We know you'd never steal from us."

"Yeah, whatever," he mutters. "Well, I'll be down tomorrow. What time?"

Because I offended him, I agree to what I don't want but dismiss it as trivial.

"Okay, we'll see you at 2:30 P.M."

*   *   *

When I get home, Bob says there's a message on the machine from Joshua. Figuring he's canceled, I'm not surprised and even a little relieved. But the message states he'll be late, so we wait. What shape will he be in this time? He could be irritable and discontent. I know I am. Addicts have the uncanny ability to walk in a room late and have you feeling guilty for being angry.

He comes in like an express train. I check his pupils as a matter of habit. He catches me and says, "What are you looking at?"

"Your eyes."

"I'm not loaded, Mom," he says, sticking his face out

and closer. "I don't come around you guys loaded." *Not loaded? Well, that's debatable*, I say to myself. His eyes don't look right to me. He acts toxic. He may not be in an acute state but he's certainly under the influence. We all are.

I try to change the subject and suggest we watch a movie. Joshua says, "You know I can't sit through a movie," but in the same breath reviews a couple of films he's recently seen. Maybe he can sit through one when he's high.

"So let's order pizza or get something." It's four o'clock and he wants dinner; I want a nap. We go get subways. Dinner is tense as his emaciated skeleton wolfs a sandwich. I sit there scowling and pick at a salad.

Minutes after returning home, he shows me a canned good from the pantry. "Can I take this?"

"Sure," I say, wondering if it'll tick his dad off, as it is a large unopened peanut butter, Bob's favorite. Some moments later I look and he's cutting up one of his father's T-shirts to make it sleeveless. "Did Dad say that was okay?" I ask, trying to disguise my anger.

"Yeah, he doesn't care."

"Dad can never say no."

"I'm not spoiled! Don't say I'm spoiled!" he says and grabs the shirt and walks out the door, cawing like a crow flapping away with the last bread crumb.

A few minutes later Bob asks, "Where's Joshua?"

"He's gone—I pissed him off when I questioned about cutting up your shirt."

"I told him he could have it. I don't even wear it."

"You wear it all the time!"

"Why did you have to ruin it?"

"*Ruin it?* I wanted him to come at 7:00 P.M.; he comes at 3:00 P.M. I wanted to eat dinner at a normal time. We buy dinner and all eat at 4:00 P.M.! I try to set limits and you collude and make me the scapegoat!"

I pout and lick my wounds. Somehow, some way, I

have to accept this. Joshua is a selfish, sick, toxic addict. He won't go to treatment. He doesn't work. He maxes his credit cards and uses and uses. His contempt for me is a projection of his own self-hatred. If he's mad at me he can use with less guilt. And Bob and I do this dance of sugar plum co-dependents or spar like pit bulls over a pig's ear.

*   *   *

Only days now before our recording session and I'm excited. The last two practices went well. My voice is strong, the musicians wonderful and the songs are coming together. As the music upped the octane, the message came through louder and clearer. This impromptu ensemble, session players hitting an easier stride…more rehearsed more comfortable, yet still new acquaintances. How is it then they mesh this music and speak its language fluently? Is it written on their souls as on ours?

Joshua will soon go back to court. He'll either be ordered into treatment or go do some think- time in the tank and come out slicker and sicker. It's none of my business. Fear used to dictate my existence and I clung like a remora, but now the pain is leverage that propels me into action. I will go on, get through and give up this boy to my Higher Power.

*   *   *

Crunch week, the countdown begins. Our recording date's approaching and I'm nervous. The weather has turned warm but a break is predicted when we're in the studio. Not just that I perform better when it's cool, but so do the musicians. What an enormous risk this involves—all the time, effort and work, riding on two days with numerous variables to mix and match.

Joshua is also heavy on my mind. Tomorrow is his court date. I suspect he's worried, although I never asked. I pray the judge orders him back to treatment and much longer this time. Although, it's unlikely Joshua is ready to work a program, rehab buys a few weeks to enjoy him. If he goes to jail, we're not sure we can visit without serenity pulled out from under us. Our recovery is not that seasoned. We wish it were but know better. We still have difficulty with in-your-face fearsome reality. We can deal with it better from afar. Of course this is all future tripping and a waste of ink and paper.

I will save my voice for the studio and fears for God. The serpent's coiled and ready to strike, but I will sing, and singing changes souls, minds and affect. I will sing with hope in my heart. I will sing my heart out, reach out and hopefully touch and comfort yours.

*　　*　　*

While in mid-conversation with a friend, the phone breaks through with another call. It's Joshua, *the* call I have waited for all day. But I'm surprised when he explains he hasn't been to court yet and it will be tomorrow. Expressing fear he says, "Mom, the world sees me, sees all addicts as wicked. They look at us like worms. It's not fair. We can't help being born this way, yet we're punished for it."

"Joshua, people fear addicts. I used to think they should all be thrown into jail too, but I no longer feel that way. They should be put into rehab, not prison. But let me tell you what society really thinks," I continue. "They think Dad and I caused you, an innocent baby, to turn out like this. We've been tried by an international tribunal. We are blamed and held responsible for a disease."

"Joshua, sooner or later everyone has heartaches. Don't judge your life by others. You don't know what burdens they carry, what demons they must slay. I'm sorry, truly sorry you are going through this, but I know some day you'll recover. God told me and I believe Him."

*　　*　　*

One hour later the phone rings.

"Mom, today's the 2nd, isn't it?"

"Yes, Joshua."

"Mom, my watch says the 1st! Mom, I missed my court date—it was today! It is the 2nd, isn't it?"

"Yes Joshua...so what are you going to do?" I ask so calmly it surprises us both.

"I don't know...I guess I'll go back down there tomorrow and try to explain."

"That sounds good. Someone who was trying to avoid responsibility would never do that. That can only work to your advantage."

"Well, I'll call you tomorrow and let you know what's up."

"Fine. Love you, bye."

I'm certainly staying out of his and God's way. I could have reminded and clarified his court date but it wasn't my priority.

I cannot do a thing except love and pray for him. Can I also visit him in jail?

*   *   *

After waiting all day for Joshua's call, the phone finally rings at 6:30 P.M.

"I just woke up, Mom."

"You didn't go to court today?"

"I can't do this Mom. I can't go on like this."

"What are you saying? Are you talking about killing yourself?"

"I gotta go Mom, gotta go; can't do this any more.

"JOSHUA! I'm coming to get you! We're going to get you to a hospital. These feelings will pass."

"Mom, I can't do this. What's life all about? Why, why do I have to have this? I'm not a bad person. I don't want to go to jail."

"I know you aren't. You're a good person with a bad disease. If you turn yourself in, it's the honorable thing and it will work for your favor. This isn't the end. It could mean a new beginning."

"I hate this. You have no idea how bad it is," he says and starts to cry.

"It must be awful. I wish I could trade places."

"Will you be there when I get out? He's sobbing now. "Can I call you?"

"Anytime," I try to soothe.

"I don't want to cry in there."

"We'll have a code—10, you're doing fine; 5, okay; 1 or 2, really down," I offer. "Do you want to talk to someone tonight?"

"No, I'm coming home. I'd like to spend a little time with you and Dad before I go in."

"That's fine, but are you okay to drive?"

"I'm okay, just scared."

"Let's go to a hospital. They can prepare you."

"No, I just want to see you."

"Okay, drive safely."

He makes it home. He's asleep right now and hopefully will turn himself in tomorrow. Should the court give him another chance? I think it's in the State's best interest to order him to treatment, but I have no authority to mete out justice or real solutions. Perhaps a few miserable months in jail might make a difference, but this is a brain disease and a band-aid won't stop a gushing artery.

*   *   *

Today's our final countdown to the studio; another rehearsal and test to live and let live. Who could have known? Why the crisis now? What am I to learn, to take away and use? This isn't coincidence but divine destiny. Swept up with circumstances that collide, its studio time, jail time; months of preparation and months of denial.

My goal is coming together; his losses culminating in consequences awful and real. Will I make it through, will he? Can I swim across the current and find a pocket and float to shore? Or will it carry me to deep depression? Where and how will God use me? Use Joshua? Use you? What is this journey, this long ride into that forbidding gulf? This turning over and turning into the wind, the fathoms stretching blue-black, calling and luring to drag us under.

What does hitting bottom look like? To Joshua, industrial strength suffering. Loss of freedom, bad food, no sunlight, friends, family or chemicals…eyes tearful, staring, rolled up and begging. Sallow grey skin over circuitry; hands clammy and shaky; palms speckled and poisoned. Bearded stubble on a gaunt face. Sunken eyes, pitiful and haunting. Speaking in whispers. Paying the price.

And for me? It is the worst of times; it is the best of times. Our recording day, our time, time we've waited for; his time, his time's up—my son facing his music, wracked by pain, doubled over in despair.

I hold back tears I cannot purge, not here and now. My voice—I must protect the instrument. I cannot protect him. I must let go and go on when I want to collapse and curl under. I must dive down and retrieve my goal and come up for air only because I have to.

* * *

A week later and I'm still coming down from the studio. What an ambitious undertaking. It was our first experience—and we rushed and recorded ten songs in twelve hours. The question is: Can I live with it? Each day I hear another thing I'd like to change, but time and money are finite currencies. As I contemplate, the phone rings.

Joshua turned himself in and they didn't arrest him, but let him fill out a *form* explaining his missed court date and assigned him a new one. Joshua feels such relief he starts the process to go back in-patient. But a few days later I call and his roommate answers. No, he isn't home, he hasn't seen him, he stepped out a couple of hours earlier. There's just enough hesitation to know Joshua is probably sitting right there coaching from the sidelines—an ominous sign his resolve has already met implacable resistance. The roommate sounds ashamed and prompted. He sounds like a classic co-dependent, the parent dodging the principal's calls.

Upon waking this morning with break-through worry, I prayed for Joshua's recovery and for someone who's battling colon cancer. She's facing a second round of chemo doing everything to avail an arsenal to fight her monster. How it must confound her and others to see Joshua disregard the treatment for his disease. Instead of meetings, *his* chemo, he courts the very thing that threatens his life. Less than two weeks ago he was dreading jail and now he's back in la-la-land, jokin', smokin' and livin' in the haze.

Tension builds and I'm compelled to check on him. I rationalize my relapse by reciting his recent request: "Mom, if I start to spin out of control, try to reason me back," but dismantling denial is disassembling the great pyramids.

"Joshua, I'm worried about you."

"I'm fine, Mom. Really. You'd think after being so scared I'd be ready, but I'm not there yet."

"I just have one question Joshua—something I need to know. Are you happy? You see, if you should die, it will help me—knowing you were doing what brought you joy."

"Yeah Mom, I'm pretty happy. I need to go."

"Fine, Joshua."

As the crazies surge and recede, I ask Joshua if he's going back into treatment. He mutters something about not wanting to hurt us, but refuses.

"I'm afraid you're going to overdose."

"Oh, so now you think I'm gonna die? I always thought you said God was gonna heal me Mom. That's just great—you know how that makes me feel? You can forget it. I'm not gonna die! And I'm not going to prison—I'd kill myself first!"

160

"Joshua, if you're going to talk suicide I'm ending this conversation."

I walk away. Bob takes over with a little schmoozing here, a smoothing over there. "Take care Joshua; we love you. Be safe, be smart. Hope you make your assessment appointment. Love you, boy."

So what a lovely set of possibilities: Death by overdose, accident or foul play, death by suicide to avoid incarceration or his complete loss of mind. Out of his own mouth he says he's too much into the life to get out and stay out. I need a meeting to get the focus back on my Higher Power, on the here and now of what I can, rather than cannot control; roll over and float, not flap in random attempts to swim the icy channel.

But the mother in me pulls me back to co-dependency. I want to drag him out of that apartment kicking and screaming, shove him into the car, walk him through the doors of that treatment center and make him get well! I want to beg, plead and reason him back. I want to beat it out of him, shake him loose from it, scream at the top of my lungs and rip the gauze from his eyes and clouds from his brain. I want to hold him so tight my nails dig into his skin and draw blood and insight. I want to save my son. Stop the destruction. Reach him in time. Keep him from dying and going out of our minds. What perverse irony: If you want something, let it go.

* * *

It's apparent he didn't make the intake appointment and now he hasn't called or answered the phone in days. His roommate relays messages and we wait. What will it be this time—a crying jag, a meek and sheepish easing back into our graces or a suicide threat on our doorstep? So much is slipping away; nothing now, except fear crouching in the corners.

The phone rings at 11:30 PM and jolts me from dreams to dread.

"Mom, I'm sorry I haven't called."

"It's okay."

"I don't like to talk when I'm loaded and I'm loaded most of the time. I'm either loaded or sleeping two, three, sometimes four days in a row. I guess God woke me, 'cause I just got up and wanted to talk to you."

"I'm glad to hear your voice. How are you doing?"

"Scared shitless."

"That's the paranoia. It affects the nervous system."

"Oh, yeah—this stuff really fucks you up, sorry," he says, apologizing for the F word.

"I missed my appointment but called and got a new one. This may sound enabling, but please, please call and remind me before my next court date."

"Do you want to come home and detox?"

"Yeah, maybe a week … I gotta do something. This stuff is killing me."

He promises to call again. I recapture the drowsiness and fall back to sleep and awake to a new day—or how does it go? "Same shit, different day."

Instead of liniment, addicts' families are salt to their wounds. By avoiding them, the pain lessens. The ones who care most are the first to go. Addicts gravitate to others in the same or worse shape. To stand in the presence of healthy norms, especially loving, grieving families, magnifies their fall from grace.

* * *

It's two weeks before the next crisis du jour.

"Mom?" I hear something in his voice but beat it back.

"Oh honey, I'm glad to hear from you!" I gush.

(Geez, get a load of me. He calls and I shimmy like a

baby bird waits wide for worms.)

"Mom, I'm really fucked up. I'm..." he says haltingly, his voice dropping to a whisper. "I'm...I'm shooting now," he confesses. "I want to die...just die."

"Joshua! Please let me take you to detox—you aren't thinking straight!"

"Naw, I don't want that; I'm just so sorry...so ashamed."

"Joshua, you have nothing to be ashamed of. Would you apologize if you had leukemia?"

"No, but if I didn't do chemo I would!" he argues. "I'm so fucked up. I haven't done anything bad yet, but I even feel that coming on—like I want to steal; naw, I don't want to, but *have* to."

"Joshua, please, please reconsider!"

"Maybe I'll come tomorrow but you'll get pissed if I leave to use," he says honestly.

"I won't be angry but concerned," I reply. "Please remember things seem awful now but you can get better. You really can."

"What am I gonna do, Mom? What am I ever gonna do? I want to die; I just want to die. I'm gonna go get drunk. I'll see you tomorrow."

"I love you Joshua."

"I love you too, Mom. I'm so blessed that you and Dad still love me. Nobody else gives a shit out here."

I want to rush to his side, hold his hand and lead him back. He belongs in the hospital and I belong with him. I'm his mother, and yet I must wait until he's ready. I must wait and watch and remain supportive but unobtrusive. The call didn't come from an emergency room but his own crisis center. It screams but I can only console from afar. The shame, a gummy sludge is too deep, too vast.

Years ago I trained to be a registered nurse. I learned patients are expected to recover or die. No one really likes to talk about that and the medical field is reluctant to admit it, but there is this pervasive, unspoken expectation: Either get well or die. Even helping professionals feel impotent in the face of death and at best can offer only palliative care.

If Joshua cannot get well, cannot do for himself what is required to arrest this disease, perhaps he too, should die.

Imagine sitting by while your children waste away. Only you can't even touch or be near them because a mountain of shame stands between you. Only now and then can you hear them call out from the crevasse, but they warn you to stay away and apologize in a single breath.

The choices are dismal. We could try to go get him, beg him to come home and go back to treatment and for a while he would get better. But it would only be for a while. Inevitably, he would relapse. The other choice is to wait for so much pain he wants to recover. But waiting may lead to his death, not bottom.

He is mainlining crystal meth. The news slices through my brain. It couldn't be more repugnant if he were drowning puppies and eating their bile with a spoon. Mothers are only as happy as their saddest child. He's sticking needles into his veins seeking more bang for the buck. He's ashamed it's gotten this bad. He sees no way out. He sees his death and is powerless to stop it and we are, too. God, please let him recover *now* or take him quickly.

Bob comes home. I wish I could keep it in and not ruin his day but I need to process. I need his comfort and support. He reads the signs. "What? Joshua? Is he in jail?" he barks. "No, more likely headed to the morgue," my voice breaking into tears. The phone rings. It's our daughter-in-law and I ventilate to her. When I hang up, Bob's missing. Spent, I fall into a fitful nap. Waking later, he's is still not home. I'm confused and hurt.

After returning, Bob marches in and doesn't say a word. My abandonment wants answers. Oh, now it's clear.

Bob can't do sad so he does mad. He's mad at both of us and masking his sorrow. He can't do scared, so he's mad. He's mad at me because I'm afraid and mad at Joshua for not trying and for making me so scared and sad. He's probably even angry at God. I know I am from time to time.

Tried and true values were in place when Joshua stepped into adolescence. He was armed and backed with love. How could anything go wrong? But wrong it was and wrong it is. Like a knife in the bottom of a back, we're all dying deaths we despise in a place called addiction.

*　*　*

I'm tearful today. Cleaned house for a while, sobbed for a while and prayed for a while. Then Joshua called. He's moving back home, ostensibly to return to detox and treatment, because he's, "out of money and sick of being a slave to the needle." We don't know if he's serious. Pain blunts discernment.

Joshua comes in resplendent and contrite. Same song and dance but the tapping is faster and the tune shoddy, but imaginative. Nevertheless, low points morph into a Pacific trench, fathoms deep and frigid with blue pressure. I try to pay attention but we both know it's an act; he's too guilty to call me on it and I'm too worn out to bother.

He looks the thinnest ever with visible tracks on both arms, which he tries to disguise with black marker pen. His face is sunken and the skin a sallow ocher. He says he's sick of people looking at him like a tweaker (a meth addict) but he is a tweaker and that's the way speed makes you look: Skin stretched over bone, eyes foreign and paranoid, the incredible shrinking addict and yet he wonders aloud how he can live in a world of mundane boredom. His options: An emaciated tweaker or a bloated drunk.

My emotions jerk from shock to repulsion. People drive by, mow their lawns, water flowers, pay bills, prepare meals and go on living their ordinary lives with their ordinary problems. Only you and I know of this extraordinary darkness that resides within the walls of a home and souls affected by this disease.

Now I must hide my purse, lock doors, set alarms and hope no one from *his* world followed him here and is bent on doing him or us harm. Warn Bob not to share razors, as Joshua could already be HIV positive, and take his photo, for God only knows if he'll be alive tomorrow. I must watch what I say and how I say it and muffle the committee in my head, which commands I should do this or that to insure his recovery. I will try to live in the here and now and relish this present moment. I will try even harder to stay out of God's way and not direct Joshua's life…or death.

Joshua's mental illness is not unlike schizophrenia. While he's on his "meds," he regains his mind. While schizophrenics are on their meds, they too often acquire stability. But also, like the mentally ill, the addict soon begins to hate the way the "meds" make him feel; his "meds," going to meetings, calling his sponsor, working the steps, avoiding using friends and old triggers. And the real insanity, identical to the schizophrenic, he doesn't think he *needs the meds.* And once again the crazies creep back, take over and take charge. Although the addict doesn't hear voices the way the psychotic does, there is that *call* that tells them to do anything to satisfy the cravings.

What's it like when they come back? I could almost go mad with grief. I'm getting ready for work and ask Bob, "Can we talk?" A minute later he strolls into the bedroom, picks up the remote, changes the channel and puts it on mute while he stares at the screen saying, "What's up?" Now I'm livid. Is he thinking, *Quick, get this over with and I'll pretend to pay attention?* He sees the anger and tries to forestall my fury. "I can listen and do something else at the same time." I stomp out of the house and jump in the car.

All day the tension builds until I return from work

and Joshua gets up. What mood will swamp the room? What will ignite him this time—or will it be spontaneous combustion? He demands to get his stuff from his friend's apartment. Patiently, carefully, my voice pinched with restraint, I explain the coming week is bad for me as I have several commitments. I see and hear the agitation mount; his irritability and mine are on a collision course. He raises his voice and I say, "Joshua, I can't do this. I know this is a crisis for you and I'm sorry, but it isn't an emergency for us. These are your problems and you cannot expect us to drop everything and rearrange our lives."

"Families are supposed to help families!" he bellows, "I'd help you!"

I think to my sarcastic self, *Oh, just when do you suppose that might ever be?*

"Joshua, I'm going to talk to you when you're less toxic."

"Oh yeah—just put me down. I have to kiss your ass don't I or you'll send me packing. That's what's wrong with you, *always* been wrong with you—you don't listen, you only CONTROL!"

"I can't do this, Joshua. I can't do this." I get up and walk away.

Five minutes later he apologizes. I don't know if it's genuine or because he's afraid of losing his bed and bath. He groans he's so sick of it. He's sick? I'm so sick I could run through traffic.

With each rehab there's an opportunity for recovery. But this implies a larger rather than smaller favorable occasion. Much like Apollo 13 re-entering the earth's atmosphere, the crippled craft had to thread the tiniest needle. One miscalculation and they would skip off into space. Joshua's trajectory is just as finite. His "window" is even more exact; one misstep and he too, will spin off and away.

When it's possible, Joshua has agreed to be evaluated for manic-depression. I've suspected for some time he is bipolar. He reports crank relaxes rather than speeds him up, and in order to calm down enough to sleep, he needs ten cups of coffee. More theater of the absurd.

* * *

Joshua passed for normal today. After seventy-two hours of detox, a shower, shave, clean clothes, no multiple earrings, tats and tracks covered, he looked like any skinny college kid home for summer. As we walked the mall, he drew no special attention and no drug dealers offered what he loves most. So often Joshua says he doesn't go "looking for the stuff," it just finds him—rationalization and empty excuses. Crank is his pimp.

Early in the disease, it's possible to disguise pathology. Injecting under one's tongue, nipples or fingernails draws no attention. Of course, as the disease progresses, the addict becomes more reckless. For a while, they can impersonate healthy norms but this too shall pass.

As Joshua detoxes, his mood swings are wider and more pronounced. Yesterday he was so low he had thoughts of suicide and then later was high as a weather balloon. Classic bipolar or is it just an addict's profile? Reluctantly he went to a meeting, his first in two years, saying he felt shy and embarrassed. I encouraged him to go and remember he didn't have to talk. What's important, meetings are his medicine.

Arriving home, he struts into the room with great pomp—clapping, hooting and happy like a yellow lab with a stuffed toy. He is jubilant from the meeting—his transfusion, his medicine already working the magic. The din splits the silence and occupies our attention. Best described by someone else, "Yesterday he was full of self-loathing, hating his 'worthless ass,' but now he's a jockey on a thoroughbred's back."

168

And how am I doing? Not so good, I guess. Bob and I have had the same argument three mornings in a row. We're irritable and restless as we swat new worries and crop bad images. Even Bob, who's blessed with a high smoke point, is losing it. As usual I haven't slept well but I'm better in some ways. I had no compulsion to take Joshua to his meeting or check up, follow or quiz him later. If he came home high we were prepared to let him sleep it off and put him out. He'd be back sooner or later.

The following day I'm with Joshua. Coming to a stoplight, the car next to us proudly displays the announcement written in white shoe polish painted on the rear-view window, "University of Hawaii Bound!" I look away to tamp the pain. Joshua forces a rude belch. I frown and think to myself, *where's he bound, jail and his fourth rehab*? We pull away and a store catches my eye. I long to shop and browse and fill the holes made by the drill and drone of the disease. Children are a license to dream, hope and renew...but my license is revoked.

*   *   *

Later the same day:

In conversation with a friend, a former addict, now in recovery many years, I ask, "When you decided to get clean, was it an epiphany? Did you just know you'd never use again?"

"Of course not. I took it day-by-day. You see, when you quit, you feel like you'll never have fun again—like your happiness is permanently gone, but taking it minute-by-minute, it relieves addicts the obligation to promise themselves they'll stay clean and sober forever."

"Oh my gosh—I think I get it. You have no idea how much this helps. Joshua says I'm never satisfied and he's right. I keep expecting him to have this clarity when he will know, *just know*, he'll never use again. What an unrealistic expectation," my voice trails with insight. I did, *do*, expect too much from him—from everyone, from myself. Maybe this is the two by four across my chin. Can I now be promoted to the next level?

Later still:

Joshua returns from an N.A. meeting and hits the house like a locomotive. "You will never ever guess who I saw tonight," he enunciates with precision. Before I can stop him, he blurts the name of a fifteen-year-old boy from our neighborhood who's in outpatient treatment. I saw it coming for years, so I'm not shocked. Kids who get caught up in drugs sometimes are easy to spot. They act cooler, cockier and more confident than the rest. They dress, walk, talk and act out in ways that at first are subtle for the untrained eye. He has all the telltale signs, but not his older, shy brother. Bob isn't surprised either, as we nod in agreement.

True enough, there's something different about kids who try and then become ensnared in drugs. Gee, I'm sorry for the family. They're in the belly this minute and isn't it obvious? They stay indoors and friends don't come over. Their blinds are pulled during the day...weeds invade their flower beds. Oh yes, they're in the darkness and my heart aches for them. I want to reach out but that would blow their anonymity. It was wrong of Joshua to tell us.

When Joshua goes on to say he disclosed at the meeting how his addiction escalated to IV use, I want to scream but dampen the thought, this is *his* problem, not mine. But true enough, I'm embarrassed the neighbors probably know the gory details if their son gossiped too. Oh, do I hear about this. Joshua rants, "You shouldn't give a shit what people think!" Unfortunately, my generation doesn't air dirty linen. After all, isn't he an unfair judge? Just a week ago, he hated people looking at him like a tweaker. To add weight to my argument, I ask him to run this by his dad, and when he does, Bob is even more chagrined. But, Joshua's right. I shouldn't care what people think and haven't I made progress? After all, I'm going public with this.

It's days like this I feel more threatened as the disease jumps on my back and stabs me with a new ice pick. The noise has quadrupled and the arguments have multiplied a thousand fold—tension, sleepless nights and hyperactivity so electric we flinch and startle.

Jason was to arrive this morning to help his brother. Of course Jason has ADD and he forgot he had a doctor's appointment, so that moved everything off until tomorrow, requiring us (for reasons that are too boring to describe) to baby-sit Alec when we had already made plans. If plans are changed for Joshua, there will be hell to pay. This latest spat left a plethora of pain. A sizeable component is self-serving narcissism. Remember, you're dealing with addicts; they will have you wipe their butts if they can get you to do it.

Joshua will go to court this afternoon for breaking probation, not following through with after-care and for underage possession of alcohol. One year ago he was as close to being free of the legal long- arm as pen is to paper.

He talked his brother into helping him get his larger pieces of furniture. All went well until I asked if he remembered the lawn chair I bought him. He forgot and I burned with resentment. At that single moment all the stuffed stuff exploded and I hissed a nasty retort then walked away. But I couldn't leave it alone and came back to spray more accelerant when he threatened he was going to get mad. Swinging my hips like I found five dollars, I replied, "Oh I'm scared, *real* scared." The irony is, I am scared, petrified of him, of "it," of repeating this sad, sick story. Later I apologized and things improved but when fights erupt, closeness is compromised. Was I intentionally provoking him out of revenge or an unconscious need to distance myself in preparation for a long jail sentence? Probably both, the disease confounds and confuses.

Last evening, Joshua confessed he thought of relapsing because he was so angry, but also acknowledged relapse is entirely *his* choice and an addict will look for any excuse to use. Joshua can use with less guilt if he can think up reasons to be mad at me. I also wondered aloud if he had unconsciously set us up by knowing if he forgot the patio chair, I would flare and give him an excuse to use. Or was I just acting out and being a picky, petty bitch? Detoxing taxes all, leaving us irascible.

Thank God for Al-Anon. I quickly remember the slogan, "How important is it?" and catch myself before throwing a complete fit. But I'm exceptionally sad. Joshua will likely spend another birthday either in rehab or jail. His first incarceration was right before his fifteenth birthday when he and three boys went joy riding. With that single event, we were ushered into legal darkness. Then when he turned eighteen, he was in rehab. And then last year, right before his twenty-first birthday, he went to jail again for the MIP. Of course the biggest event, four days in jail, was when he was eighteen and drove drunk and crashed into a car with two people.

But, today is a good day. He is clean, sober ten days, going to court, signed up for rehab and seems stable. He doesn't know if it's because he's less toxic or just ready to comply. We shall see what God has in store for him and I must remember and ready myself. It is for *him*, not me. It is his sentence, not mine. But I flash back to those metal doors at the juvenile detention center—a place of baby gangsters, neophyte felons and parents poisoned by pain.

*   *   *

Joshua gets a slap on the wrist. The judge sentences him to classes for two weeks and then to rehab in Spokane, Washington, a ten-hour drive from home. The system is overwhelmed; Joshua must seem like a low risk.

I'm worn out but what was dreaded no longer chills me. Joshua's presence has been disruptive and for the greater part, an immense aggravation. I love him, but no longer enjoy him. To be in his presence is like living on an international runway—jumbo jet after jumbo jet taxiing one after another. He electrifies the room with shooting sparks, attracting yet repelling those intrigued but terrified. There's only silence when he's asleep and even that's fitful. It's difficult to sort his toxicity and our lowered resistance. Probably both are factors. At any rate it will be sad to see him go, but also a warm and welcome coverlet.

If drug addiction was an infectious disease, the Centers for Disease Control would mount all efforts to punch a hole in this plague. Could a cure be forced amnesia? Wipe out euphoric recall? Or would that be too costly a solution? How do you put a price on pain? In four point restraints, the tension tempts me to give up. Hearing Joshua talk about it makes it worse. I don't have to have it in my face to know it's real. I'm not in denial. I know how bad it's gotten and how much he loves it. No amount of warning, begging or chiding will affect an iota of difference.

Joshua barges into rooms, streaking through the house bulldozing conversations, slamming doors, stomping, cursing, shouting, drumming, moaning and groaning while clapping, howling and bellowing at the top of his lungs, strutting with wild, dry-drunk bravado. Frantic, I run to barricade myself in the bedroom.

Everything must come to a screeching halt for the addict. Everything is an immediate crisis that must be addressed, fixed and validated *now*. He reports with sobriety the cravings grow stronger. With abstinence, the promise of higher highs pulls his attention.

We have only two choices—turn him out and live with the consequences or live with the consequences without guilt. We're under siege, another foot soldier on the disease front. Hold on! Hold on, my soul pleads. He will be in treatment soon and you will have him back from the dead. Focus on that, not this. Loving children is grand, if we can be in their presence without wanting to scream.

Better day, better self-care. I worked and worked out and Joshua was gone for ten hours. We both needed the break. He did his first day of Day Jail and came home tired and relaxed. Thrusting the phone into my hand, I'm taken by surprise when he orders, "Say hi, Mom." Thinking it's a girl I've never met, I make a flimsy attempt to play along when I discover it's Joshua's oldest friend from sixth grade—a sweet kid, now sounding remarkably grown up. He recently purchased a house and he's only twenty-one. I gush congratulations, chitchat and wish him the very best and also invite him to stop by some time. He sounds confident and sure. He had been a quiet pothead once upon a time. Now he's worked a good job for several years and arrived safe and sane into his twenties. Without a twinge of envy, I feel nothing but happiness for this nice kid.

Joshua goes on to announce another friend is playing football for the University of Washington—a senior at a PAC-10 school, a boy who wasn't as good a student or as talented an athlete. Now I fill with grief. I wouldn't take a thing from the other kid, but it breaks my heart Joshua's disease stole so much, so soon. It's one thing to have heartaches and who doesn't have them? But most know it later; not so early. Addiction robbed Joshua in his sunny youth. It pulled his life out from under him and replaced it with a lie, a lie that licks its lips and laughs in his face.

*   *   *

"MUSSIE! MUSSIE COMMADINI!" Joshua shouts as he clamors into the room. What was once cute, affectionate gibberish from my little boy now seems absurd.

"Joshua, stop acting like a baby! You're an adult. This is ridiculous; you're almost twenty-two."

"SORRY!" He hollers and waves me off then turns with anger. "I'm not gonna change for you, I'm gonna be myself," he warns.

I counter with undisguised relish, "Well, I'm going to be myself too, and I want to talk to a man. I don't enjoy your company when you act like a fool."

He leaves the room and I embrace the calm, but a nagging thought whips me back. In what ways do I bank or douse his recovery? I'm afraid I love that little boy who was silly and boisterous. But the real-life, stunted, selfish addict is a stranger I do not like or even want to know. What I've seen is too scary and over-the-top for my ordinary, provincial self. I'm coming up through awareness as if pushed from behind. Where once I was clawing out, now an unseen force propels and flings me free.

*   *   *

It's been sixteen days since Joshua moved home and last night he relapsed. Now he's forced our hand. Now what do we do? Hold that hard line and throw him out once he comes down, comes back? Give him one more last chance? Just what do we do?

Of course setting and keeping limits is important, but what if he throws himself at our terrified feet? What then? The age-old conundrum: If addicts are sick, is it humane to kick them out? Humane or cruel, necessary or punitive—the lines are blurred, a recurring struggle with the counter-pull.

We set our boundary and he knew the consequences, which may strengthen, not weaken his resolve. But if we give him another chance, he could possibly complete Day Jail and actually make it into treatment, which is exactly what he needs. Sixteen days of turmoil. We opened the door and let it stroll right in. Once again we put down our lives to contain the firestorm. Offering temporary asylum, we held onto elusive hope that maybe this time would be different. But of course, we were wrong. The crushing cravings ignite the underbrush. Will he die with a needle in his vein or a bottle in his lap?

* * *

Not one word from Joshua. Addiction reminds me of what I heard on T.V. this morning: "The U.S. East Coast announces the 'Summer of Sharks' after numerous sightings and attacks. Defiant swimmers ignore the warnings and go back into the water."

At first I start to sink but catch myself. Prayer and a meeting beat back the voice that tells me I caused him to leave. I remember I'm not responsible; he was gassed and idling at the curb. This is what an addict does. I don't have to catastrophize; I can reframe this. Without these episodes, why would he want to recover? If he misses Day Jail, they will arrest him. He'll be back in trouble, not on his way out. If he doesn't go to treatment now, maybe he will later and maybe later will be better.

My immediate concern is to notify the authorities before they arrest him on our doorstep. I'm on hold for eight minutes and then finally connected but quickly cut off. When these little things happen I see them as a clear sign to go in another direction. With confidence, I take off early for a walk and picnic with friends. I return home and the house is still standing and my life isn't in ruins. In fact, it's quiet once again. Joshua is out there very sick, very out-of-control, but I'm riding the waves and taking care of myself. Although ensconced in parent purgatory, this is temporary suffering. I think I'm finally learning how to stay just ahead of the pain.

There's a message on the machine from Joshua saying he's okay. He'll probably finish Day Jail and then try to ease back into our graces, like we even care at this point. If he goes to jail, rehab, whatever, it's all such insanity; at this place in time, I'm too tired to bother.

I watch a television special about a woman whose daughter is a heroin addict and has been in and out of rehab six times—nice kid, nice stay-at-home PTA mom and loving dad. But the kid still becomes addicted—once overdosing and almost dying. The mother confesses for a second she is relieved, yes, *relieved*, when her daughter nearly dies. Because, with her death, God forbid, it would at least be over.

The phone rings—its Joshua sounding awful, crawling back, not to stay he says, but to get his things. I'm cool and detached. Not to worry if you can't detach with love, you'll detach from exhaustion. No, he can't come over. He can't come near the house because he hasn't been to Day Jail and they are looking for him. We don't want a Swat team zooming in with drawn weapons. When he squashes the warrant and has a bed date for rehab, he's welcome. No, he can't have his stuff. He should have thought of that and packed better when he left to use. This is not a bed and breakfast for a practicing addict but a safe haven for someone clean and detoxing.

A few minutes later he calls again, "What am I going to do—where can I go?"

"Jail, Joshua—turn yourself in and do your time."

"I'm not doing THAT!"

"Fine, do what you do," I say, as we both hang up in unison.

So what's the worst that can happen? More of the same? So. He actually changes for the better? Great, but unlikely. Or he dies? For just a micro-second, wouldn't you feel relief? Slowly I've sloughed the sorrow replacing it with a harder edge. My sympathies are shrinking. I used to stumble through these crises but now I'm driving the bus. And yet...I dreamed last night Bob and I were murdered and buried under the house.

Karla Klear Sky

178

EIGHT

Chop Shop

2001

How do you live when your life is in embers? This disease is punishable by death. As one prepares for the marathon, the subtext speaks the deepest destitution. Agile and light footed, the monster's finest talents break the sturdiest souls. The dainty death-watch waits its turn and neatly pecks us clean. Where opponents are closely matched, contests entertain, but unequal battles hold little appeal except for the thugs who enjoy them. But far beyond this blood bath we see that addicts cannot exist as others do. They have to have something different and that something is a mind-altering drug. They seem incapable of facing life on its own terms. Maybe Joshua's relapse can be the jarring experience that brings a more rigorous recovery. Who understands the alchemy and ingredients in the mix?

Someone asks at a party, "What does your son do?" I answer with pallid prevarication, "He's self-employed in leisure and entertainment." Translation: He's an unemployed addict who hustles. Lies block truth and exodus; couriers delivering packets of painful but important reminders.

* * *

I postponed writing today and committed to additional work that will delay the manuscript. Writing is automatic, so I suspect this stall is as futile as stifling a sneeze. Now I question every motive in every matter reaching for the inner meaning. I suspect this tarrying is propelled by fear, the common thread of my life. As I tease the tangles, am I afraid I will be the chaff or Joshua? Will that be the ultimate discovery, there's nothing worth salvaging? Or am I slowly learning to forgive the mistakes we've made and detours as essential?

I mustn't put off the book. I was appointed to write, which is much more than a curse, but a hybrid that leaves deep divots of doubt. But I must train my pen. I'm an abductee transported to this outpost that commands indentured service. As I answer the call, it demands the truth. Parents are waiting. I hear their cries in the night and their footsteps as they pace. I see their sad eyes stunned in disbelief. A mother hears the music; sees the book and takes it home. She turns the pages and they lift her from dark places she thought she only knew.

The father, blanched with grief, longs for comfort, but doesn't know where to turn or how to reach for help. He bears it silently and marches on while he struggles with a man's private sorrow.

They wait alone, crucify themselves and pound collective fists against the evil. They sit in silence and disappear as their children self-destruct and their lives explode, "fractured," as someone said, "yet tethered to a freight train that hits them hard and drags them for years."

*   *   *

Joshua's twenty-second birthday came and went yesterday, the second birthday for which the disease separated us. He called in response to our earlier greeting but we were in the studio finishing the mix and missed him.

I can grieve or be grateful. He is still alive and I can remember those first thirteen years when he was well and we were too—those precious years when he was our dear young son, loving, full of promise and close attachment. When he would, as a big boy, crawl into my lap and cuddle and talk and nuzzle my neck. When he would say and do the dearest things, for he was the dearest of children.

It's nine days (and yes, I'm still counting because he still and always will count) since Joshua left. Now I wait for it to unfold instead of frantically forcing solutions. I wait for it like the surprise of an unknown, not the anticipation of a dreaded certain. I cannot predict the future and the future may hold wonders waiting to be seen.

Joshua left a message saying he's safe but how absurd. He said he loves and misses us and wishes he could have "both." Equally absurd is a question from a loved one who lives out of state. Over the phone she asks, "So Karla, have you *really* emphasized how this is killing him?" I barely contain patience with the platitudes, but go on to explain gently with three excellent rehabs and after-care, Joshua has the tools to fight it. But knowing and doing are galaxies apart. Recovery is possible only when addicts are ready to enter that personal wormhole, which transports them across their inner darkness. If they think about drugs, they don't have to think about anything else.

* * *

Washing out the garbage can on the front lawn, I notice in my peripheral vision what at first I refuse to see—a sheriff's patrol car slowly inching its way towards our house. My first instinct is to drop the gushing hose and run and hide, but a strength I can't call my own forces me to look up and face what approaches. *This is it*, my inner voice warns, when it answers with uncommon confidence, *you can do this*.

Because there is only one officer in the vehicle, my hunch suggests this is a cursory attempt to locate and arrest Joshua, not notification of next of kin. My eye catches the sheriff's and we both nod polite hellos. The sparkling, toothy grin against his young black face promises a benign encounter. Quickly, I look down as he creeps past our house searching for a different address. I busy myself trying to appear normal as he turns and drives away—carrying my relief. The disease plaits heavy braids of paranoia.

My heart skips when I hear Joshua's voice. Each one of his calls is special—but troubling, too. It's been days since I've been able to reach him, not merely hear a message on a machine. A remnant of resentment hangs like a skin tag but I divert my attention from it. Yes, he calls when he wants something, and when we're able we always pick up, but we are not afforded the same courtesy. I must remind myself he's not in his right mind and a mother's memory is short and forgiving, soft like lemon curd.

We chat and I toss out one or two reasons to reconsider detox. I do this more for myself than him, knowing full well it will be met with resistance but pad my conscience should I be wrong and God takes him while I'm not looking. I know it's impossible to redirect addicts; they have lost their editing function. Their cognitions are filtered through a scrim that distorts competent reasoning. One cannot shrink-wrap them into protection.

* * *

Weeks pass and the World Trade Center, White House and Pentagon are targets of destruction unequalled in our country's history. Thousands die and are injured. This is the first time since 1938 the FAA grounds all flights in the United States. Only yesterday Bob and I flew back from California. We missed the onslaught by hours. Bob's wallet was lost and we feared his identity and perfect credit were also stolen. How quickly our problem seems minor when lives are extinguished in a few monstrous minutes.

Pain comes in countless, cruel ways. Even now thinking of Joshua puts his possible death in greater perspective. Joshua is one sick, unproductive, unrecovered, disinterested addict. In all likelihood he slept through this calamity. Who besides us and perhaps other families of addicts would understand? When I think of the multitudes who will grieve, will it help me when and if Joshua dies? Why should my grief be more caustic? If anything, shouldn't

182

it be less? Isn't that what the world believes? Life is full of suffering. Parent pain is only a piece of the pitiful pie, and special pain isn't very special when bodies rain out of the sky in deaths too awful to imagine.

Later in the day:

Joshua's cell phone has been disconnected. I can't talk to him, see him or even leave a message. I don't know where he is living or if he *is* living. I'm sad today—sad for America, the world, for everyone looking for answers. I'm sad for those who have died, are dying, will die, for those buried under mountains of debris and for my child and yours who have the means to escape addiction and yet, when they are almost free, turn and go back. I mourn for the souls who didn't have a choice and feel their dismay. I try to remember my addict and yours are sick and disoriented, dazed not only by the concussion of their disease, but the organic inferno in their crippled minds. Some will survive and recover. As those souls lie in the darkness, they hold on to that faint hope. I pray for those buried alive under buildings and those in the rubble of addiction.

Fear drapes me in a shroud of jeopardy. Are we prepared for our personal and imminent destruction? Hijacked long ago, are we now locked and positioned to realize the final implosion? Am I not allowed one last call to tell him how much he mattered, how much he was loved? Mysterious musing: Was Joshua paranoid or clairvoyant? Remember when he said 9:11 was a bad sign?

*　　*　　*

Twenty-seven days since I've heard from him. This is the longest and most disturbing stretch. I'm troubled in a way I've never been. Something is different and more ominous. Just thirty days ago he was motivated to finish probation and go in-patient. How quickly life becomes hopeless, exacerbated now that I have no way to talk to him.

Fear stabs me in the shower and slashes until I brace against the tile and slide to my knees. Crouching on all fours, gulps of air in staggered breaths struggle through curtains of rushing water. Tears gush and taunt. Is he dead? I fall back against the wall, rest my head on the soap dish and clasp hands and pray...

> Catch me when I fall oh Lord,
> And help me make the climb.
> Hold me when I'm cold and shiver deep inside.
> Wrap your arms around, and tell me all is well.
> Touch my hand and kiss my cheek
> And stay until I drift to sleep.
> Shoo away my fears and lock them in a vault.
> Whisper in my ear—reassure it's not my fault.
> Rock me when I'm hurting and hum a lullaby,
> Pick me up and prop me up before I surely die.

I open the bathroom door and there's a message on the phone. Oh, thank you God. He's *still* alive. Prayer *does* change things. The message is brief—his voice low and nearly a whisper. He sounds depressed but says he loves us. He doesn't give any indication of where he is or how we can reach him. There are no pleas begging forgiveness, and yet, could it be a suicide note? The thought transcends fear, a little tickseed I will blow into the wind.

*　　*　　*

A week ago the world witnessed the terrorist attacks on the United States. Regardless of one's personal beliefs, this evil crossed a line that compels a collective repugnance; a point of no return where humanity will rise and roar with such resolve, it will change the course of history. Crossing lines control destinies that permanently alter the here and now and the forever after. Joshua crossed a line many years ago and entered that new and dangerous space.

A letter came from him three days later, great relief and greater understanding, too. He has made his decision and has no desire to find his way back to the other side.

Dear Mom & Dad,   *September 19, 2001*
    I felt like writing you guys this morning because I miss and love you a lot. I just wanted to let you know I am safe and not in danger. I still...have not gone into any negative old bullshit. I just find a way to get everything I need.
    I'm in Seattle but I do not have service any more for my cell phone. I do have a pager. Call me anytime you want on that and I'll get back to you. I mean it, anytime you want, you're welcome. Oh yeah. If you wanted to do the nicest thing, you could mail my clothes and stuff. I will call you soon. I love you Mom and Dad. Enjoy every day and be happy, please!   *Love, Josh*

What insanity. He believes he's safe and not in danger. He jabs needles into his veins and shoots street speed straight to his heart. He believes he's safe because he *must* believe that in order to stay in denial. He goes on to reassure us he hasn't resorted to stealing and hustling pads his conscience. So far consequences are palatable. Having made his choice long ago, crossing the line was his mistaken rite of passage.

He makes it clear he wants to keep in contact but follows the butter-up with a request as usual. Having paged him twice last night, it is clear his best intentions are meaningless. He never returned our calls. He ends his letter with an appeal for us to take care of ourselves. Can we strive to have a normal life without one eye trained on him? Hasn't he given us permission? We've contracted despair but in that circle too, is a quiet place of devotion; with that, we can choose to stay on our side and love him from afar.

But the world of addiction is a funny freak-show, a universe of smoke and mirrors. Hope evaporates with fear like soap bubbles on air currents—silent; unpredictable—plans and promises are puffs from the village idiot.

Joshua calls asking to come home again to detox. His intentions are vague and no doubt dubious, but we agree to another attempt. Just forty-eight hours ago we didn't know if he was alive. The saga is slippery quicksilver. Fears are more ferocious and good signs always suspect. In the words of someone in recovery: "Will this latest attempt be another spit, pop and sputter? How soon will he squirt through our fingers? When will he next be remanded and ordered back into the custody of his cravings?"

The second morning and the stupor dissipates but the aggression steps in and steps up. I cringe as his detoxing brain comes to terms with reality. He's in our house facing jail—clean/sober time—and we are watching and waiting from the wings. We stand, as someone describes, "in rotating shifts, but it's like keeping our eyes on a hockey puck." As he finishes breakfast, I mention we expect him to call his probation officer.

"I'm gonna shower first," he growls.

"The only reason I'm saying this is I thought you might go back to bed, which you did yesterday."

"I know I have to take care of this bullshit!"

It's clear he's here for R. & R. not because he's serious. It's impossible to disarm the rocket.

He pops his head into the den to say he'll call the probation officer later. I reply, "Fine, but we will follow up and check."

"Do I lie to you?" he questions with eyes shooting sparks.

"Yes Joshua, many times."

"Well, how long? How long's it been? It's been a shit-load long time! I don't lie to you any more!"

186

"Joshua, I don't know how long it's been. I'd have to check my journal."

"Oh yeah! My whole *life* is documented!"

"Joshua, I've learned to trust behaviors and that's what I'll verify." He bristles but I remain chilled like pastry crust ready for a hot filling.

Later in the day, he finally calls the probation officer who recommends squashing the warrant. Joshua announces he's not interested in meetings and will stay with friends until his new court date.

"That's great, just great," I say as the air crackles with tension. "You come suckin back, sleep and eat and now you're ready to take off—typical."

"I'm outta here," he says, and starts to pack.

"DON'T DO THIS!" I yell, sweeping my arm across his dresser and knocking every last thing onto the floor. "WHY? WHY?" I screech, choking on tears and pushing the end table over toppling the lamp. "ANSWER ME! ANSWER ME!" I scream and sail a shoe across the room.

He grabs his jacket and heads downstairs. "Joshua, this is not in your best interest," I say, following and crying harder. "Staying here, staying clean, going to jail and in-patient is. Was it something I said this morning?"

"I don't know."

"Joshua, please don't go," I say pulling his arm and sobbing…"I'm worried that…"

"That I will *die*," he says cutting me off.

"Yes, you'll drink today and stick a needle in this vein tomorrow!" Wailing, "PLEASE, PLEASE RECONSIDER!"

"Mom, I love you," he says turning around, "but I'm just not ready. If I should die, remember I was doing what I enjoy."

Like rock climbers, addicts fall in love with dangerous suitors that tempt them again and again. But sometimes their harnesses break and they fall into God's hands.

As quickly as the argument starts, he's out the door and gone. I swear I won't be caught in the net but before I wriggle free, I'm speared with hooks and hacked with machetes. I devote so much time to a disease that impersonates my son. It's a hobby for morons. I collapse in a puddle and howl at the moon.

*　*　*

Coming down for the first time in nine months, or is it nine years? The CD Release Party is a success, a perfect day considering my recent brush with despair and this late date in fall. Ordinarily we'd have cool, rainy days but God's grace once again showers us, not with rain, but sunshine.

The house is wall-to-wall with people and the chaos and confusion make for a wonderful time. As the adrenalin kicks in and backs off, everyone loosens up except for me. I'm flying on nerves and can't calm myself. In a few short hours I will bare my soul and the thought terrifies me.

We begin the presentation and I introduce the musicians and give them their CD's along with a little gift. They are gracious and seem to appreciate the spotlight. Bob and I kept them waiting for nearly three months to hear the final mix. All seem pleasantly surprised. To top off the evening, I pay a special tribute to Bob. As he starts to tear, I look at this wonderful man, the love of my life, and thank God for him. We play the CD and show a video of our time in the studio with some of the day's party thrown in for fun. Afterwards and most spontaneously, some friends ask for our autographs, which tickle us and pleases the musicians.

The afterglow settles and a couple of people disclose their struggles with alcohol. It is an honor they reveal such intimate details. I feel immense gratitude.

All this puts me in a good mood. The following week, as a pre-emptive strike, I talk Joshua into getting hepatitis vaccines. Wish there was one for hepatitis C. I have to agree, however, not to lecture, nag or mention anything related to recovery. To sweeten the pot, I buy him lunch. Although agitated and grouchy, he seems satisfied he can follow through and do something that pleases me. I tell myself this is a feasible and worthwhile goal.

How unnatural to pretend to not notice his greater weight loss, not comment on his poor hygiene, not grab him and hold on for dear life—his life—his life that slips through our fingers. Seventy-eight percent of all IV drug users eventually go on to acquire hepatitis C and HIV. With the possibility of such deaths, a quick overdose seems preferable by comparison, but …he wouldn't die in our arms.

Joshua contacts us again, I think in response to an earlier message I left about wanting to build happy memories. He agrees he'd like that too, and then slips in the real reason for the call. It isn't just to talk, but a request as usual. He and his roommate are out of food and can I bring groceries. I mention food banks and how sorry I am the disease takes so much. Also, gently adding anytime he's ready to get well, we are waiting to help. But we cannot and will not bring groceries. I want to add, but prudently don't, *just how do you get cigarettes and drugs if you're flat broke*? I have to admit he doesn't get ugly or argue, but the icy wall erects its barrier between us. Now he's over the phone call. I tell him I love him, but he doesn't return the sentiment.

He still doesn't realize his worst day clean will be better than his best day using. At times I'm afraid of recovery. Tasting triumph would make relapse a more bitter pill. The tease would tempt me to grab too tight, and if it were torn next time, I might also rip apart. The present pain is familiar, a level I can stay on top of so it doesn't sweep me away and drag me under.

Last week we celebrated our thirty-second wedding anniversary. When I think back to the six and a half years we chose to live it up before making babies, I shake my head how we fantasized about our unborn children...how we planned the perfect family. How naïve.

I sat across from Joshua and looked at my baby now all grown up and so screwed up. He was wearing a short-sleeved shirt making no attempt to hide a visible track and I told him how upsetting it was. He dismissed it as a scratch, convincing only himself. Try as I may, all encounters are flecked with pain.

For the last two days, Joshua has been here and slept forty-six out of forty-eight hours. He gets up, gobbles carbohydrates, smokes a cigarette and falls back in bed.

When he first mentioned he wanted to come home, he said he missed us, but I knew there was more. I knew he had lost his bed and bath at the most recent friend's apartment from where he was evicted. Tired and hungry, his visits are only R. & R.

When he arrived, I hugged his bony skeleton, which reminds me of Steve McQueen in the movie, *Papillion*, when he sticks his shrunken head out of solitary confinement and asks another inmate, "How do I look?" Lying, the guy answers, "Fine...just fine," knowing the poor bastard's almost dead.

When Joshua rouses from his three-day crash, the next stage will be pleasant but less peaceful. He'll be cheerful, noisy and loving. But after another couple of days, he will get irritable and discontent. The visits are little more than a stop-and-go along an infinite byway coming from nowhere and going no place.

Earlier than expected, Joshua takes off this afternoon to stay with a new friend. Re-energized, he's raring to go and do his thing. Along with him, my sadness and resentment tango out the door.

Later, I discover he took one of my best sheets when I gave him an old one. He sleeps and eats off us for five days, and this is how he honors hospitality. An ember blazes as my fury flashes fast and furious. I page him twice, knowing the futility. The fiend cackles from the shadows.

Two hours later:

Joshua finally answers the page. Holding back, I calmly ask rather than accuse him of switching the sheets. He swears emphatically I'm mistaken. It's just at these times I question myself and back down. Oh, it's not that important, except an indication of lack of trust, which he points out. Perhaps I do jump to conclusions, and wasn't I still angry about the recent R & R? True on all accounts. After a lot of back and forth, I acknowledge I could be wrong and he validates my frustration. He admits the second he is rested, his feelings come up and he wants to escape—troll for thrills and obey the crave. God help me be a better mother to my addict.

From now on, I will document, cover my butt and use Bob as a material witness. With two unreliable brains, both chemically altered, one due to menopause, the other due to toxins, it's really a toss-up.

Next day:

I find the sheet I accused Joshua of taking. Paranoia is a milky cataract. I make amends, swallow my pride and gulp a piece of humble pie. I wear an Estraderm hormone replacement patch on my abdomen. I should slap it on my forehead and get to a meeting.

* * *

Travels, like heartaches, take us to far corners. Caravans cross long distances in the Sahara Desert searching for salt, a product most valuable and as precious as gold. Boys, age nine or ten, sometimes accompany their fathers on the arduous journey for the adventure, the experience and

191

preparation for adulthood.

Parents carefully explain to the young boys the dangers and temptations that await them in the desert. Fathers describe in detail if a child should ever wander away from the caravan, he must constantly check the horizon in order not to lose sight of the camels. If the boy loses the caravan, it's unlikely he'll find his way back and will disappear into the blistering expanse.

To assure the caravan's survival, they must not, and will not stop and search for a missing person. But in spite of serious warnings, many youngsters are lost to the desert. The dunes beckon from all sides to lure them away. For some, the call is too great, and they drift and are swallowed by sand and sun.

Imagine the anguish of a father when he discovers his child is missing. Every instinct tells him to save his precious boy. But he knows to leave the caravan puts him also at risk, as well as the family back home who depend on him. He cannot ask the caravan to stop because that places everyone in peril. He has no other choice but to grieve and move on and keep moving on. That's life in the Sahara. That's life in general.

As the caravan returns, the desert leaves its hardest test for last. But the travelers give abundant thanks for their survival. And for the child that perished? He was not the first to be lost to the desert, the first to vanish into scorching sands.

The disease, like the desert, may claim our son's life. But we who endure intense, protracted pain, can follow it to our own oblivion or keep moving on to a new oasis.

*   *   *

When Eric Clapton's little boy fell out of an open high-rise window to his death, I tried to imagine how one comes back from that edge. How does a parent go on when their child plunges headfirst to their demise?

Filled with dread, I call Joshua this morning hoping he will take care of my fears as he dangles in the down-draft. I barely finish hello when he cuts me off, "I'll call you back." First thinking he's on another line, after a half hour it becomes glacier clear I'm interrupting a high and calling back will take a few days. Fearful and angry, I leave a nasty-gram. But later call a second time with amends should he fall out the window and off the ledge forever.

* * *

Tomorrow is Thanksgiving, and most likely it will be the first ever our son will not be with us. Contact is more sporadic as he orbits behind the moon. Or could it be he's on course for re-entry and experiencing the blackout? Will he burst from space into the blue-white of recovery? Or will he burn up and disintegrate in complete and lonely silence?

While getting dressed for work this morning, I notice the clothes I set out last night. Everything was chosen in shades of black. Slathered in sloppy sorrow, I do it again and call Joshua and insist his friend make him answer the phone. Joshua is crashing off crank making it difficult to understand his speech. It isn't quite a slur, but choppy, wake-like turbulence.

Under the spreading sick disease the village nitwit stands, I ask foolishly if he's coming for Thanksgiving. "Naw, I don't think so, besides you know I don't like to drive that far," he stammers.

"Well, we'd really like you to be here. We can come get you," I press.

"Mom, I love you, but I'm just real tired and I'll be sleeping. I really don't want to go into a lot of details."

"Joshua, I don't want details, I just miss you. Everyone misses you, and this will be the first Thanksgiving you've ever missed," I say without guilty intent.

"Oh yeah, go ahead Mom—lay your shit on me. Don't you *get it*? I'M AN ADDICT! I feel like an outcast! I love you, but I just don't want to be around everyone!"

"Joshua, no one treats you like an outcast. We love you."

"I know, and I love you too but I just need to sleep. I'm really tired and I'll be more tired tomorrow. Tell you the truth, I didn't even know tomorrow was Thanksgiving."

"Can I ask you something? How do I ruin your high when I call?"

"Mom, I don't want to get into this. I'll call you in a couple of days."

I tear up but hold back in silence.

"Hello, hello?" he says, a little irritated. "Mom, I love you. I'm just an addict. I will try to call more often. Call anytime you want, okay? Okay?"

"Fine, bye," I say quickly before blowing my cover. Hanging up, a flood of happy memories sweep over me in waves of tears—remembering the good, now more painful than the bad. Slowly I must adjust my expectations. Joshua most likely will be absent this holiday and all that follow *if* he survives. We cannot, and will not have a normal life with this disease. According to a recovering addict, calling when Joshua's loaded is like, "Pissing on his high," a high which cost him money and now brings him down. No wonder he isn't eager to chat.

* * *

Thanksgiving morning,   November 22, 2001

I cried myself to sleep last night and have awakened less sad, but more bitter. My son is only forty-five minutes away but unable and unwilling to show up for Thanksgiving, show up for life. I believed my children were gifts from God and took that job seriously—maybe too seriously. If they did something worthy of reprimand I would swiftly respond. But how does one chastise a disease? I gave parenting one hundred and ten percent, but now, when I want to cash that check, it's returned and stamped "insufficient funds."

194

But instead of dwelling on the losses, what can I be thankful for? Much, if I will stop feeling sorry for myself and pay closer attention. Joshua loves us. He's not coming because of hate or cold indifference, he's not coming because that's what active addicts do—they stay away from families when they are toxic and full of shame. I'm grateful for much and must remember all that is right in my world. I have a wonderful husband who loves me and is truly a great man. I have children who love me, extended family, food, shelter, sufficient income, meaningful work, friends and health. I have a good and abundant life. I can walk and bathe, dress and feed myself unlike the time my joints were swollen triple and red with revolt. Serum sickness, some doctors said, after six days of Premarin. There is no way to know for sure unless they challenge me again and that would prove I'm allergic to mare's urine. But the answer could also leave me wheelchair bound for life. Other white-coats thought it was environmental, arthritis or some freakish autoimmune thing. Whatever it was, for several weeks I was a physical cripple and even today the arthritic grind reminds me I dodged a significant bullet. Thankful? Oh yes, I have much to be thankful for if I will sit and listen to my body, review the past and pay attention to my present.

Thankful too, my Estraderm patch provides the hormone replacement I need but bypasses the liver preventing complications. Hopefully it protects my bones and heart without causing my breasts to break out in cancer. Baby boomers are the guinea pigs of the generation. We'll either live to be a hundred or all drop like flies at the same time. I hope we haven't padded the pockets of drug companies at our dismal expense. But hey, I was talking about thankfulness—and like Scarlet, in *Gone with the Wind*, I'll think about that tomorrow.

Recovery compels one to confront and conjugate one's life. Now better prepared to slosh through pain, the abyss is nothing more than a shoal. I can roll up my pant-legs and wade in. I will not only slice and dice but also carve up resentments into manageable bits to chew and churn and then turn over. Keener consciousness is rich like a dream.

I heard that one of the "Sandy" dogs in the musical, *Annie,* was rescued as a puppy when it was found with a collar embedded in its neck. The poor animal was fearful and aggressive but with tender care, she learned to love and live without malice. She learned to be thankful.

*   *   *

It's the day after a major holiday without Joshua; nothing but the leftovers from Thanksgiving dinner and a family chewed by this disease. But as I pray, I thank God for what is good in my life. Trying to remember too that acute, corrosive pain will pass and recovery is suspending disbelief. The task appointed is to focus on the current pulling us toward our destiny and remember too, we're all swimming in grace. Tucked in the shade of a majestic tree, we kneel and give thanks. Bending like palm fronds, we surrender.

*   *   *

Spoke with Joshua today. I can no longer tell him what he wants to hear or grant a full pardon. He parked illegally and his car has been impounded. It will take $150 to get it out. He hints he'd like us to help, however we will not intervene. His car will go to auction this week, but we're not fighting and falling apart. The disease ends up taking everything. Like an earthquake, it causes cracks in foundations and aftershocks come—not in days, but decades.

A few hours later he calls again asking when we're going to see him. What adorned utterance this time from the pink-tongued skink? I play along but I'm cautious too, for he's a polished sycophant. Seconds later he reveals the real reason for the call. He has two bags full of laundry and it's

196

time to visit the parental unit and cash in on some freebies.

Calmly, I tell him we'd be happy to pick him up at the bus station but not if he's going to sleep and graze, then take off without visiting. He counters, "Well then Mom, you're gonna have to teach me ahead of time what a real visit is."

"You know exactly what I mean."

"Well then bye Mom." Without a moment's hesitation I flash, "Bye," and we both hang up. It feels good to set a boundary. Just four days ago it was Thanksgiving. He had plenty of laundry then but other business. He will rationalize he doesn't need us like he doesn't need his car, apartment or anything else. He sold everything and put it in his arm. That's how he will support the addiction. It's all part of the disease and process. Acceptance may be the ticket but you can't take the ride without standing in line. Nothing I do or don't do will change his fate, but I've had to find that out for myself, as he will, too.

*   *   *

While donning the protective facemask before tossing my head back, a chuckle rumbles from under the paper shield as I gaze at Bob also performing his bedtime ritual at the bathroom sink. As I squirt Minoxidil onto my scalp, to stave off thinning hair, I ask, now lisping from white teeth strips crowding my mouth, "It's gotten bad, hasn't it?" and we both break-up laughing.

What a gift, what a nice surprise, to accept aging with humor and perspective. What might have seemed daunting, I roll off and tuck into that special place for little problems. Bodies remember what minds repress.

Looking back to 1990

When you're six feet tall, over forty and a female American Caucasian, walking into a train station alone in Dongduchon, South Korea, attracts attention and surprises. As I wait for my husband and our sons to meet me, I reflect on the challenge we have thrust upon ourselves. We didn't have to join Bob, an executive Army officer stationed there for a year; in fact, families weren't authorized on short tours. But some young wives were brave enough to buck the system. Few, if any, were my age. Did that make me more courageous or enmeshed? We tell ourselves it is love and adventure.

We live in Tokerie, a small village twelve kilometers from the DMZ in a tiny, two-bedroom apartment, substandard to anything American and/or familiar, without an oven, dishwasher, garbage disposal, washer/dryer or car, we tough it out for the year. We haul potable water from Post to cook meals and brush our teeth and oftentimes to flush the toilet when the local system shuts down for days. Nothing compares to losing that utility—not heating oil, not electricity, not even transportation. Water. Water is the most precious commodity. We learn quickly to keep the tub full and buckets to the brim. Even braving blizzards waiting for dirty buses dim in contrast.

Looking around the bleak and bare train station, I feel more alone than ever. At least when we lived in Germany I could blend in, but now I'm in a sea of small brown people who stop and stare.

Chilly as usual this fall day, I push my gloved hands deep into my pockets and hunch a bit to ward off the cold. Although Korea, for the most part, is a friendly host country, some young hoodlums resent the American occupation. Slicky Boys, as they are called, target U. S. citizens to rob and plunder. We are fortunate and avoid the thieves by always leaving lights, radio or T.V. on when we are gone. It's incomprehensible for Koreans to waste electricity or anything else; therefore I'm sure they're convinced we're home, when we're not.

When in foreign countries, we always try to fit in and thwart threats of any kind, from looking and sounding naive to outright assaults to person or property. However, one day we take a family hike in a mountain park and while minding our business, teenage punks rush past and one of them pinches eleven-year-old Joshua and runs off laughing. A big, red welt quickly rises on his little arm as he falls to the dirt and cries in pain. We want to wring the assailant's neck, but he's fast and disappears.

While in the cold train station, that memory reminds me how alone I am and how different I feel in this strange and distant world. Deciding to sit and make myself less conspicuous, I watch people smoke, sneeze and spit into their hands and wipe them on their clothes. I see women carry huge plastic bowls of cabbage on their heads ready to pickle into Kim Chi while mothers yell and slap children or pace and soothe babies wrapped onto their quilted backs with satin blankets. I smell cauldrons of larvae that waft putrid in the air but even more rancid odors emanate from bathrooms. Young and old, farmers, businessmen, women dressed in modern suits and shiny spiked heels wait to board the train for the one and one-half hour ride into Seoul.

I notice too, a tiny old lady who sits at the far end of the terminal dressed in traditional garb—loose-fitting slacks, heavy jacket, no hat and turned-up slippers. Her face is worn by sun and sorrow. As she slowly stands, the years and burdens stoop her. She shuffles, but moves deliberately towards the bench where I sit at the opposite side of the lobby, when it becomes clear she's approaching me. Bracing, I watch more with curiosity than fear. What can this little woman do? I can eat soup off her head. As I contemplate the possibilities, she continues across the tile floor and stops within inches and looks into my eyes. I stiffen when she makes her next move.

Bending over, not with the characteristic head only, but half-body bow, she slowly rises, extends her hand and offers a stick of gum. Her warm smile and crinkly face says she remembers how her country suffered and appreciates Korea's ally. Jumping to my feet, both surprised and ashamed of the earlier doubt, I return the bow and thank her in her own language, accepting the gift and public gesture.

Can it be this disease is serendipitous? Little sunny surprises await us at every turn. Recovery requires me to amend my life in order to propagate a new future. I must remember I still have a future, unlike those killed in brutal battles such as the Korean War. Problems are possibilities to learn more about ourselves and the life we want to live. I've stopped thinking of them as punishments meted out in unpredictable doses, but opportunities sprinkled from heaven. Contentment is a choice.

* * *

We have worked out an unspoken agreement. When Joshua calls, we will bend over backwards to make the time pleasant. We will try to not say things that disturb him, and he will try not to incite an emotional riot in us. Lots of love yous, miss yous and hoop-dee-doos as we pretend the dragon is snoozing.

Although the disease coats my heart in sorrow, I calm my restless observance. We don't know if Joshua will recover, for now there's only a dollop of hope. But we've made up our minds to preserve what's left of the relationship because of our abiding love.

But the smartest enemy attacks where you think you're safe. Jason has a possible career-ending back injury due to a ruptured disc. Seven years of United Parcel Service seniority and now he may have to start over somewhere else. But I'm bulletproof. This is small in comparison to other horrors I conjure in my mind. As his brother sits and shoots street speed in Seattle, this is a bump in the road.

* * *

Joshua will be here for Christmas. What do you buy a homeless addict? Should it be grocery certificates, fast food coupons and bottles of vitamins, shaving cream, toothpaste and things that will fit in his backpack or stomach? Certainly not clothes, he doesn't have a closet. Money? Not a chance. The disease changes *everything*, even the gifts under the tree.

The day after Christmas, we have a conversation:

"I love you, Mama."

"I love you too Joshua."

"You okay?" he asks, hearing something in my voice. "I just want my mom to be cool with me." As Joshua lies on the sofa, I sit down next to him and place my head on his chest.

"It's okay, Mom. It's gonna be okay," he soothes and pats my back.

"No Joshua, it's not okay. We can make believe it is, but none of its okay," I say in a whisper while my ear is pressed to his heart and my face turned from his. Now looking up into his eyes, I go on, "I'm worried about you. You don't look well."

"I'm okay. I'm feeling better today," referring to how awful he felt yesterday when we picked him up. He's clammy and shaky. His face pale and gaunt...the light faded in his eyes.

"I just never really feel good," he admits.

"I know. Your color is so bad," I say out loud. "It's gonna be okay, Mom," he says as I get up and move to the recliner across the room. "Don't stamp me dead!" he yells. "I'm not gonna die—I will not die!"

"Joshua, I know it's hard to hear anything that challenges denial, but you know this will kill you," I start to lecture but catch myself. "I'm glad you're here; thanks for coming."

"Oh yeah—cause Josh might not be here next year."

"No, I was actually thinking about a friend's son who said he was coming for Christmas and then backed out the last minute," I say, not taking the hook.

"Well, good for him! At least he's living without guilt."

Now circling the bait, "I thought you wanted to be here," I say with tears filling my eyes.

"I do, but you just like to lay a lot of shit on me."

Now neither of us speaks and remembers to obey the rules. I must accept this reality that intrudes on every day and every holiday. I remember our sick son made an effort to be with us on Christmas.

After the dreary pause, Joshua appears melancholy. Inquiring what made him blue, he shares how he longs to have his own place again, how he hates moving from friend to friend and surviving on the street. "Mom, you know how organized I am. I just miss having my own room."

"It must be so hard," I answer, full of compassion.

"You have no idea," he says, the pain chiseled on his face, a relief forced by cruel fate.

NINE

Clawing Out

2002

The beginning of the year holds hope to make and keep resolutions. Joshua announces he's ready to give up drugs and backs up the claim with a good faith effort to return to court. He says he wants to come home, but won't be a meeting thumper, already blowing his cover.

What we think might be an attempt to seek asylum while fighting the war, turns out to be another scheme to squat and collude with the enemy. Calling him on this, he's guarded and defensive. He agrees to stay clean but will not go to meetings. I suggest he might be trading one addiction for another—in this case, alcohol as his midseason replacement. But a drug is still a drug and another ramp to nowhere.

I run this by Al-Anon friends to see if these are boundaries or another form of control. Originally the contract would be: Clean and sober, adhering to court compliance, seeking rehab, meetings and no incoming/outgoing calls.

Points address motives. Are these decisions and boundaries to make life easier or to help encourage his success? If it's for us, that's a boundary. If it's to force a solution, that's control. And most importantly: What do we want? We don't want the turmoil but don't want to slam the door on him if he's trying. Torn as usual, it's gray with many unknowns.

Going to court first was a positive sign, refusing meetings, a very bad sign. But whether or not he works a program isn't our business. Phone calls at all hours are. So now we're in a stall. Unbeknownst to him, we probably will let him return as long as he shows progress. We love him and are prepared to try it as many times as it may take. He's worth it, but so are we. If it gets too crazy, he'll want to escape before we order his eviction. Tiresomely uniform, we brace for the next kick in the solar plexus.

But there's a quiet interlude and reports of progress. Turns of events keep our hopes piqued. Joshua is living with his brother happily and has a second job interview tomorrow. It will be interesting to see how long this lasts. Life with an addict is always a challenge.

Co-dependents worry and obsess. Everything seems suspicious that threatens peace. Even good things are suspect when bathed in radioactive paranoia. The faulty thinking tells families they can prepare in advance for awful news, and with that preparation, trauma can be better tolerated. But worry will keep one stuck in a fearful future and cloud the pleasures of the present. Turning it over and working the steps brings one out of the dread into the gratitude of the here and now. This is a slow and arduous process but possible with diligence.

I've spent nine years watching this disease take us down, but now I'm busy reaching for the light. As I flutter kick to the surface, breaking through and shaking despair, worries are shoulder dusters not oxen yokes.

The remedy? Theories abound in the great social and professional arenas as to why addicts are the way they are. As ideas are thrown out, some will stick and some are almost too ridiculous to repeat. Joshua's assessment with the latest erudite Ph.D., fruit, flake and nut, implies our son is allergic to peanut butter and metabolizes that in a way that manifests addiction. This flies in the face of rational thought and empirical evidence. When Joshua wasn't doing drugs, he did not exhibit bizarre behavior. He worked, paid bills, went to college and regularly ate peanut butter...the more ridiculous and absurd, the better for the addict who will embrace any foolhardy idea to reinforce denial.

For now, Joshua has given up illicit drugs but pretends he can drink like a norm. He'll get a little job and transition back into the mainstream. Of course, he won't go to meetings because he doesn't need *that*, he just has to make sure he doesn't have a peanut butter and jelly sandwich.

I'm closing the door on sorrow. I have the means to live, not merely survive. Recovery allows me to do other things and grieve and give it a proper burial. Like a tongue compelled to reinvestigate a chipped tooth, I was driven to revisit the hole in my soul. But now the lessons are eulogies that honor the old and give hope to the new. I'm reminded of the joke about the little girl Anna who was in the restroom on a train. The conductor was striding through the cars, calling out the next stop, "Dunanna, Dunanna!" when the poor little thing on the pot answered, "All but the wipin."

*   *   *

I told my story again at another Al-Anon meeting. I didn't rehearse but spoke from the heart. I also sang four of the songs along with the CD. I messed up the first but pulled the rest off okay. Singing, like writing, has become a self-inflicted pain-fest. But I believe this is God's plan and He will restore my confidence so I can carry the message with poise and grace.

A recovering addict with eighteen years clean was in the audience. He told me how the police rescued and threw him into prison for five years. He also mentioned how his parents were wise enough not to enable and exacerbate the disease. But more importantly, he spoke about the power of prayer and how he battled back on the slow road of recovery. He didn't want to offer false hope, but some hope, any hope is better than no hope.

Joshua has been hired full-time at a video store within an easy bike ride from his brother's house. I think this is the fourteenth job he's held in six years. Gratefully, they have become indistinct. He goes back to court tomorrow, just two days before starting work. How this unfolds will be interesting. He feels confident being employed will work for, rather than against him.

He was destined for more but the disease insists on what it defines. He reports he is clean but admits he's not sober so all bets are off. But I shall continue my hike. Will it be a new dawn or a chilling epitaph? My objective is to stay in my business and out of his, hoping for the best but preparing for the worst; not stoned on fear but sustained with real here-and-now serenity. Today a guy swerved on the freeway and flipped me the finger, but without so much as a flinch I said under my breath, "You can't scare me, my son's a meth addict."

* * *

Are you sick and tired of this down and dirty disease? Is there little to distinguish one day from the next as they meld into an undifferentiated blur? Are you ready to hitch a ride out of here? If so, stick out your thumb and say ahh! Or as my mom, Vivian said, "Have a happy life and don't let anything or anyone get you down."

TOOLS FOR PEACE AND SERENITY
Mind your mind – Reframe negative self-talk with positive affirmations.
Set boundaries – Say no and mean it. Take care of yourself without regret or guilt.
Detach with love – Remember to honor them by letting them live their lives and experience the consequences.
Say what you mean – Mean what you say. Manipulation is unhealthy control.
Pamper your mind – Remember you don't have to suffer the reactions or actions of others. And you can act rather than react.

Harness your heartache – Honor your pain and grieve as necessary.

Gift of gab – Seek professional help and/or attend Al-Anon or Naranon, call a friend or family member. Listen and share. Work the steps.

Write it right – Journal or write your own story.

Worry time is wasted time – Create a God box. Put your worries down on paper, place inside, pray and then walk away with assurance.

Light candles – Set aside time to reflect, meditate, pray and relax.

Practice counting your blessings – Write them down. Review regularly.

Take walks and country rides – Stop and smell the roses. Fill your spirit with fresh sights and sounds. Exercise until your brain fires happy endorphins.

Pamper your body – Take a guilt-free nap, bath or shower; play music loud and dance or quietly saturate yourself in a tranquil setting.

Turn off the telephone – TV – Computer – Create a time when you won't be seduced by technology that interferes with rest and relaxation.

Reset your compass – Review your morals and values. Make a mental note where to improve.

Forgive and move forward – Go easy on yourself and others.

Surrender the problem – Imagine the problem is already solved and sit back and wait for completion.

Live your life as if – Do what you'd be doing if this disease wasn't part of your life.

Do it your way – Remember every journey is unique as you are.

Now in recovery, tools are instruments to absorb, integrate and operate from deeper awareness. Each revelation is a signpost that strengthens my conviction. I'm on the right path. How about you?

* * *

Joshua didn't skate this time. He will serve nine days in the county jail. He jacked this judge around one too many times and his time is up. Good, I guess. He seems appropriately tense and uncomfortable with the idea. Jail is especially difficult for a meth addict; the days will be long as these nine years have been.

He's determined to keep his new job that hasn't even started, already jockeying to find someone who will step in and sub the few days he's gone (as if his new employer will be so accommodating). Addicts believe if they think it, it will become fact. Their narcissism convinces them everyone will be as motivated to meet their needs as they are. He reports with time served he has to make only two more probation appointments and a review and then he will be scot-free in May. If he were clean *and* sober, working a program, that might actually happen but the disease is progressive and let's not forget, he's a *real* addict.

Addiction is savage. It invades every race and stratum of society. And when it affects a child, parents hold their breath and cross their fingers. Some kids recover but some practice as adults eventually succumbing to the monster. For those parents newly initiated to this fraternity—or for others convinced their lives are over—please remember, *you can recover even if your children don't.*

So how am I? I'm happy to say just fine. Tomorrow I'm attending a ladies' luncheon I look forward to and will enjoy. I won't have to plaster a smile on my face or forge a day of strained pretense. I don't have to hide nor do I want to. I feel a peace and acceptance that could not have been imagined nine years ago. Although buried up to the eaves in pain, in the center of a dry heart is a surprising nugget of gooey hope. Unwrapped and served on a platter of new prospects, it rolls from side to side and sticks to all the places that were forced into extinction. I may not be exactly where I want to be but thank God I'm on my way and not writhing on the floor. No longer conscripted, I can wish him well, love and let go. Next to every thorn is the rose.

*   *   *

Progress is enjoying life even when your child goes to jail. Joshua's employer responded to his honesty and promised the job when he gets out. Ironically, her son is facing the same thing, which may account for her compassion. Isn't it amazing? Recovery allows me to try something new, like plugging in the phone tonight.

*   *   *

Joshua served his time in jail, survived the boredom and came out pale, but primed for a new turn around. He's working, staying clean and talking about returning to college, saving money, getting out of debt, buying a car and even buying a house someday. But he's still drinking, so what real chance does he have? As long as he bathes his allergic brain in chemicals, he will suffer the campaign of growing madness. It remains unknown if he can save himself from himself and prevent a premature obituary. Like most serial killers, the disease befriends its victims before it turns on them.

The squalid sight of a child sinking shocks every well-intentioned parent. But as I've thrown back my shoulders with remembered confidence, I'm crusted with courage. No longer constrained, I am what I am and so is my son. Our lives may entwine but we are separate and original. Now is the time to mend our threadbare hearts. "Mom, I'll love you forever and ever, and that's a long ever," Joshua, age five.

From time to time it's good to slip away to a quiet cove cushioned from the traffic of this disease. Drawn to that call, Bob and I go to a beach house for rest and relaxation. Like a tranquil oasis, it casts its spell the moment we pull into the drive. The winter wind beats the shore and whips the waves into a frothy soup. I sink into the soft sofa poised by the picture window and solitude washes over me. Inhaling the beauty, seagulls glide and dot the stormy sky as brave fishing boats chug home in the churning surf.

Peering through the pane, the sea shears the sun over the rim leaving shimmering shadows reminding me the light doesn't leave us, we turn away from it. Like this orb traveling space, there's ample evidence patience promises tomorrow's safe return.

EPILOGUE

Timeless

"All men should strive to learn before they die what they are running from, and to, and why." —Henry David Thoreau

While drowning in despair, God proposed to me under water. With His prompting, I've learned to ask and answer hard questions.

Who was I then and who am I now?

For nine years the mask allowed me to continue with my life. It enabled me to heal the deepest wounds from the inside out until I could safely remove it and accept I am the mother of an addict. The mask was held in place but could come on and off in seconds, covering the pain. But I realized I couldn't level this behemoth. I couldn't tunnel through it or go around it but Karla Klear Sky could claw out and make peace at its rim.

I'm done with suffering. How about you? It's time to examine what was important before and see what's important now. I will no longer let this direct my life but share what I can to comfort you and others. What started as a battle to save my son has resulted in awareness I can save only myself. As disappointment fades and faith breaks the stranglehold, I now accept his life in revolt. Slowly you too can stitch your heart together by grieving, processing, forgiving, accepting and finally surrendering.

I'm going on with life. When I find myself dwelling on the past or fearful of the future, I yank on my backslide and ask myself, "But how is your *now*?" Yes, there's part of me saturated in forever sadness, but I've locked it away and only take it out from time to time. It no longer dictates my purpose. It no longer commands my undivided attention.

For nine years we were in hibernation, held captive in the belly of the beast. It takes copious strength to withstand the weathering that parches and peels hope, but I'm reclaiming my life and YOU can, too. Recovery isn't heady but quiet assurance. Now armed, I can suit up and ready myself to manage the monster when it resurfaces—and it most likely will. But I too, can rise up with a mother's mighty fury to meet the challenge and prevail. For having been to hell and back and hell again, the fires have tempered my resolve.

We have stood vigil by Joshua while he battled back, having seen him rebuild and detonate in place. We have peeked over the rim into the clear blue future and have wallowed in the bowels of this gutter disease. We have felt it tug and pull us from one another, and yet we go on. The call is faint but reassuring. If others can find peace, we too can be among them. I've decided I can rail against life or exalt it. I can moan in misery or sing my heart out. And I can finally tell myself and believe, "It's not about you."

The most difficult experience holds a perfect plan. Although it was an amputation of the soul and the phantom pain demands a scratch from time to time, that was then and this is now. And this new reality holds great promise and no doubt, future sorrows. But as I ascend that majestic mountain cruising the updrafts, puffs of poofy clouds festoon the alpine sky. Wildflowers unfurl like a baby's pastel blanket and beckon me onward and upward where the air is crystal clear. Peace waits for me and holds my place until I make the bend. The hush is music to my soul. A sacred silence rolls in gentle ripples as I prepare to listen and learn the purpose of my journey. There we surrender to our destiny, designed and sculpted especially for us, perfect in its wisdom and patient peace.

With the sorrow diluted, it no longer demands the voice to write, the heart to long, the soul to sing its mournful song. Words are humble endeavors, but hope is what I offer and I give it with all of my heart.

"Hope is the thing with feathers,
That perches in the soul
And sings the tunes without the words
And never stops at all."
—Emily Dickinson, December 10, 1830 – May 15, 1886

Karla Klear Sky

LATE BREAKING NEWS

April 2009

Joshua is twenty-nine years old, HIV negative and has been gainfully employed eight years with no legal problems. However, in April 2004 he requested a leave of absence and entered his fourth rehab.

For sixteen months he earnestly worked a program of recovery and was clean and sober. He attended several meetings a week, did service work, had a sponsor and purchased his first home. He excelled in his career and we enjoyed a close relationship.

However, in August 2006 he relapsed and decided in October 2008 to enter his fifth rehab but has recently relapsed again.

We hope and pray he will return to his program. But even if he doesn't, we will work ours.

Karla Klear Sky

216

Made in the USA
Monee, IL
23 September 2020

43258640R00135